The Coming Crisis
Answering the Call from Sinai
In a Time of Chaos

Miles R. Jones, PhD.

Published by Benai Emunah Institute
Kerrville, Texas

© *copyright 2020*
Miles & Michelle Jones
first edition

The Coming Crisis

Answering the Call from Sinai

In a Time of Chaos

Table of Contents: page:

Preface	6
1) The Prophetic Voice	8
2) Covenant at Sinai	14
3) Secularization of Education	26
4) Crisis in the Public Schools	46
5) 'Progress' of Progressive Reading	53
6) The Accountability Wars	65
7) The Call from Sinai	75
8) Conclusion	94
Appendix A – Book Reviews	105
Appendix B – Bar Mitzvah Programs	113

Preface

My journey to faith was that of a scientist. Although I was a lackluster student throughout my high school years - when I got out into the world it was different. I took off and traveled widely. Languages were no longer the dry and dusty details of textbooks to be memorized. They were the key to being a part of life in another country, as opposed to the tourist seeing that culture through a plate glass window - unable to understand, participate, or appreciate it. It turned out that I had a real talent for learning languages that was definitely not apparent in the classroom.

I learned Spanish and French, saw the need for more education and soon went to college to study linguistics. I spent eleven years in higher education. This time I applied myself with a will. I graduated with three degrees in languages and linguistics, including a doctorate in Bilingual Education. I taught overseas for some years but eventually I was called to return to the United States and go into the school system. As I relate in this book, it was a divine call, a divine calling to find out not only the problems but also the solutions. There in the inner city schools was the problem, and there, I was told, was the solution as well.

Even though I had a doctorate in Bilingual Education I was technically not *'qualified'* to teach. One had to have a teaching certificate. I got a teaching position via the Alternative Certification program, since the schools lacked enough teachers in certain areas like bilingual. I taught during the day. Every night and all day Saturday we had either hours of additional instruction or college courses we were required to take. Sunday was the only time I had to do the homework required of those courses. Summers were no different. It was intense! After two years of this I received my teaching certificate.

I did not stop there. Once I was, officially, a certified teacher I had only to take a test to add certification in different areas. I was already certified in Bilingual/ESL pre K - 6th grade. To teach secondary (high) school I had to transfer to an upper level class for the requisite teaching experience. I began to chew through the Teacher Certification Tests like they were peanuts. I studied hard never taking any of them for granted. I became certified in secondary French, Spanish, mathematics, history, and geography. I have taught many of these subjects from elementary through high school in various different schools within the education system.

Still, it was not enough! The schools were a disaster. Anyone could see that! Why? That was the question. I applied myself to studying the instructional methodology, testing, and educational philosophy of the school system. I studied these issues very seriously and in-depth for more than a decade while I was living them in the classroom. I ended up as a university Professor of Education - where I examined the teacher training process from the inside out. I knew the problems. I had even found the solutions to the problems and implemented them successfully in the challenging inner city classrooms where they worked beautifully! But there was one thing I still struggled to understand. **Why?**

Why would well-educated, well-intentioned teachers, teacher trainers, administrators, and professors continue to use catastrophically bad methods and materials for instruction. Why would they do that when the research that these methods did not work was clear? Why would they do that when research-based methods that did work were easily available? Why would kind-hearted teachers and administrators continue to literally destroy the futures of millions of children - year after year, decade after decade? Granted, most teachers do not read the research. However, the professors, and teacher trainers, are charged with doing exactly that and they were leading the way - right over the cliff! Despite all the research, and despite the impossible-to-ignore proof of failure staring them in the face, they continue. **The whole system - from pre-K to university - moves all together as one - like lemmings to the sea!**

I sat with this burning issue for many years! I had been sent for exactly this reason - to find the problems, to find the solutions. I had modeled the solutions, taught them at university. Everywhere I was opposed, my results doubted, criticized or ignored, my career destroyed. The system does not suffer this kind of rebellion. I was in a tenure-track position. If I kept my head down for five years and did not teach my student teachers such heretical things as early, systematic phonics, I would be granted tenure. After that, a tenured professor cannot be fired. I had a decision to make. What does it do to you to live a lie for five years?

I decided not to find out. When I was laid off after two years, for being "*out of the curriculum*" it came as no surprise. By then I had finally faced the answer to my question, "*Why would the entire school system skip down the primrose path to destruction?*"

There is an evil intelligent force that leads us into destruction if we choose to follow - if we do not have a firm dedication to truth! There always has been. His name is Lucifer!

Chapter One
The Prophetic Voice
August 8, 2020

Except for *The Prophetic Voice*, this book was written about ten years ago, as the final chapters to *The Writing of God* - the book that published physical evidence of the truth of the seminal event of the Old Testament, the Sinai Covenant. So why publish it now? Are there not more urgent things to do in a time when the world is disintegrating around us? As this book goes to print - the riots in Portland are in their 100th consecutive day. Nor has the extensive rioting elsewhere died out. It is just not covered by the media. In addition, other things are occurring so strange that it strains credulity to believe they are happening.

Public monuments of George Washington, Abraham Lincoln, Frederick Douglass, and Christopher Columbus are being torn down by mobs along with those of Confederate generals. Federal court buildings and police precincts are literally under siege. Rioters in some places are openly carrying weapons.

Yet, in Saint Louis, a couple are being prosecuted for bearing firearms in their front yard to deter a mob of rioters who had just broken through the gate to their private community and were aggressively threatening them with violence. The response of the authorities was to seize their guns rather than arresting the rioters. Elsewhere, a shopkeeper is under arrest awaiting trial for shooting at armed burglars who broke into his store at night. The burglars have gone free with charges against them dropped. In many cities large numbers of violent prisoners are being released from jails and prisons under the guise of preventing the spread of the coronavirus Covid-19. Many district attorneys are refusing to prosecute rioters.

Meanwhile, rioting continues apace without any attempt to enforce the law against destruction of property or even to stop savage attacks upon civilians or police. Those who are detained are released the same day, often without any charges filed against them. Those who reopen their businesses during the coronavirus lockdown are prosecuted while those who burn businesses are not.

Homelessness is rendering American city streets filthier and more diseased that the slums of Calcutta. **Crime is skyrocketing in the cities while many politicians are responding by slashing police budgets - bowing to the rioters demands to '*Defund the police!*' as a misguided means of ending racism!**

All this has supposedly been sparked by the Black Lives Matter organization and the truly fascist anti-fascist movement of Antifa upon the death of George Floyd under police custody. **How did this happen?** That is what this book is about and why I am publishing it now. The mainstream church's response has been to roll up into a fetal position. All of us are holding our breath – hoping and praying for the madness to subside.

Unfortunately, **the madness is not going to subside but rather intensify!** The current embers of rioting will be supplied with new fuel and they will burst into raging flames all over the country once again. If not before the presidential election - then surely after it. **Donald Trump will win big in 2020**, much stronger than in 2016. Ballot fraud will soar to astronomical levels! It will be evident! It will be proven! Most of the media will not cover it. Big Tech censorship of social media will become draconian in the next few months. Right now it is all or nothing for the radical left! **This is August, by November 2020, to the rallying cry of a stolen election, armed insurrection will begin in many cities across the country!**

We will witness the tragic implosion of some of our major cities! Many city economies have already been broken by the never-ending coronavirus lockdown, destruction of businesses by the riots, loss of tax revenue, and the dramatic rise in unemployment. Many city dwellers and business owners will simply shut down and walk away. Police and social services (schools, sanitation, utilities, food supplies) will be drastically reduced or even disappear. **There will be famine in the devastated areas most affected by riots! Massive emigration to the suburbs and rural areas will ensue** - bringing many of the problems to the doorstep of those presently living in secure communities. **It will be a violent civil war, and a very strange one! Some regions will be peaceful - others in constant turmoil.**

Many state and regional economies will boom, initially anyway, taking over from the failing industries of the cities. Much manufacturing of everything from steel to medicine to lawn chairs will be mandated to return from China and be done in the United States. Other regions of the nation's economy will cave - primarily in the large cities! **Israel will go to war against Iran.** Taking advantage of the coming crisis, **China will go to war against the United States in all ways short of military,** for the time being! The coronavirus may have escaped accidentally from the biology labs in Wuhan, China - but releasing it upon the world was a political decision!

As a result of this massive movement for racial justice, young white radicals have poured into black neighborhoods to participate in the protests - which often end in the burning of businesses many, if not most, owned by black residents of the community.

The young white radicals scream 'Racist!' right in the face of black policemen and women trying to stop the rioting. The blistering invective coming out of their mouths and the blind hatred in their faces negate their purported motive of seeking racial justice - remember they are screaming vitriol at black cops – accusing them of racism, degrading them, and provoking them to commit retaliatory acts which will be used to justify upping the ante for rioters to commit even more violence. **I have seen this before!**

While researching racial injustice I once came across a series of vintage photos so profoundly disturbing I cannot ever erase them from my mind. They were taken in the South during the early 1900s. They showed the lynching of a black man by whites. You can see the legs of the hanged man in one photo and the faces of the white people all around his corpse. Their faces are seething with a cathartic fury of hatred! It was like the daily ritual of group hatred of enemies - required of all citizens - in the novel *Nineteen Eighty Four*, a totalitarian future vision of our world written by George Orwell in 1949. The unbridled hatred on the faces of the people in the photo of the lynching impacted me like a bullet! In front of them is a young girl in a neat little dress no more than six years old. The blind hatred on her face is a perfect reflection of that on the faces of the adults participating in this murderous hate fest.

That little girl is all grown up now and is on the streets of Portland burning black businesses and churches, rioting and screaming curses and taunts of *"Racist!"* in the face of black cops! More likely it is being done by that little girl's children or grandchildren - shaped and programmed by the universities into the New Age zombie warrior crusading against racist violence by committing it! The blind hatred radiating from their faces which we see in the nightly news is a perfect reflection of their forebears.

The fact these young radicals, both white and black, have zero self-reflection of their actions is a warning we must not ignore! Blind hatred is always the spark of mob violence. Our children are being used as stormtroopers to implement a new totalitarian regime. History repeats itself. It is once again okay to go into black communities in force and burn them down! As long as one is doing it to end racism, of course!

Few of them have any clue what is going on. Nor does the population at large - **but I have been there before!** I was a radical of the Sixties. Some still remember the extensive highly destructive riots of the late Sixties and early Seventies. Large parts of our major cities were burned, beginning in the black neighborhoods and spreading outward. Sparked by activism against the Vietnam War the protests and riots morphed into the civil rights struggle with the successive assassinations of John Kennedy, Robert Kennedy, and Martin Luther King.

While a young man living in San Francisco I was trained as an activist and Peace Marshall to organize and oversee demonstrations and intervene to prevent violence from breaking out. Joan Baez, a talented and popular singer of the era, had dedicated a retreat - now called Esalen in Big Sur, California - to teach humanistic alternative education for the problems facing society. There, in the mountains, I was trained in non-violent protest organizing and intervention. Although we were loathe to dwell upon it, all of us were aware that there was another training going on somewhere – this one on the martial skills of violent overthrow of government and society, how to provoke violent protest and use it to one's own ends. **That end was totalitarian in nature. It always has been. It is the sweet siren's song of utopianism.** if only everyone could be forced to think alike we would usher in the workers' paradise, or whatever. Now, of course, it is the paradise of racial justice. **In actual fact, it is about seizing power!**

I marshalled many demonstrations. One day President Nguyen Cao Ky of Vietnam was flying into the United States, scheduled to speak in the city in support of the war and I was there early in the morning to organize the protestors. The first two to arrive on the scene were already in a foaming state of rage, swearing and screaming and smashing bottles. I knew then what would happen. The streets of San Francisco were filled with violence and tear gas that day and many other days. In the riots of 1968, those who wished to join in the turmoil had only to go up to the rooftops and see what part of the city was burning that day. The players behind the scenes used these protests to incite violence. Enough chaos and the people will be terrified, confused, and in doubt over their own beliefs. Such a citizenry is ripe for manipulation. Laws can be passed and actions can be taken in the chaos that would never be allowed by a sane and sober citizenry. Those riots spread worldwide. The current riots already have. **It is not going to go away! It is going to escalate!**

It only took only about six thousand radicals to take over the Russian government in the Bolshevik Revolution during World War I - which started as a protest. The key to success is having the right people in high places ready to seize the levers of power when the chaos peaks. It is to that end that many of the generation of Sixties radicals have dedicated themselves over the past decades. It has been a long march of infiltration into all the major institutions of our society – schools, universities, unions, media, charitable foundations, corporations, courts and bureaucracies. **The long march always begins with taking over education!**

I went in a different direction from other Sixties radicals. That path led me to salvation. It led me into the schools to find solutions to the crisis in education. It led me on a scientist's journey to faith. It led me to find the physical evidence of the truth of the Bible. My search for God led me down the ancient paths to the inscriptions at Sinai and the lost and forbidden manuscripts of *The Hebrew Gospels*. It has led me here to this moment - this brief moment we have to catch our breath before the deluge. We are in the eye of the hurricane. We can take this moment to find ourselves, to repent and reinvigorate our faith, to decide who we are and what we will do when the tornado comes to our door. We can join the faithful remnant of believers clinging to truth at any price - or be blown away like dry leaves in the hurricane wind which is coming! *May you make that decision now!* **May you hearken to the ancient call from Sinai – the education covenant.**

There is a plot to take power. There are Marxists in the upper ranks of those orchestrating the mayhem - but most protestors would not consider themselves such. The leaders of Black Lives Matter are avowed Communists. The website of Antifa explicitly states their overarching goal is to achieve world-wide Communism. These power seekers are not democrats. They have taken over the party to achieve their own ends but they do not have a democratic bone in their bodies. They are totalitarians. This has been planned for a long time now. If Hillary Clinton had won the 2016 election it would be a done deal. Hillary wrote her master's thesis on Saul Alinsky, the master tactician who wrote *Rules for Radicals* in 1971.

Hillary's master thesis has vanished, of course, but I cut my teeth on *Rules for Radicals* at university. And yes, I did receive college credit for being trained in the tactics of radicalism. In the past elections, George Soros spent many millions of dollars electing radicals as district attorneys in numerous states and cities.

That is why we now have the spectacle of thousands of violent criminals released from prison - and the revolving door of city jails where violent protestors are taken in the front door and walk out the back door free and clear.

Major corporations have donated upwards of two billion dollars to Black Lives Matter and Antifa in the past few months. Many of the leaders of the present turmoil are right out in the open - from politicians to celebrities to corporate CEOs. But there is one leader, in particular, whom you should know about.

In the preface to *Rules for Radicals*, Saul Alinsky wrote his acknowledgement: *"**To the very first radical known to man who rebelled against the establishment and did it so effectively that he at least won his own kingdom – Lucifer!**"*

The Sinai Covenant is the key to understanding it all. It is the portal we must pass through to give our children, and ourselves, a Godly education. It is the secret to the outstanding success of the Hebrews throughout history. It is the Call from Sinai that has made humankind literate - and the rejection of it which has rendered generations of American students functionally illiterate. The Call from Sinai is as relevant today as it was when Moses came down the mountain with the *"writing of God"* on the tablets of stone. We can listen. We can obey.

This book is for those who want to understand how we got here and how to do something about it. It is a history of our educational system and all its ungodly follies. It is a guidebook to those rational souls, *'scientific minds'* one might call them, who are seeking faith without abandoning their intellect. It is a map for the challenges we must take on to restore our schools and our nation.

It is not any sort of attempt to rationalize the miraculous nature of God. It is a call to believers to grasp the living truth, the bread of life offered by the Savior - rather than the stale wafer that we have become accustomed to in our churches. **If we are to save ourselves, our families, and our nation - there must be revival and that begins with education, the root of the crisis that is upon us!** For the root of the crisis will also yield the fruit of the solution!

So, shall we begin?

Chapter Two
Covenant at Sinai

And the tablets were the work of God,
And the writing was the writing of God,
graven upon the tablets.
Exodus 32:16

The *writing of God* - alphabetic writing - was a technological, as well as an ideological, tool. It was also a weapon. The Israelites' conquest of the promised land was the first ideological warfare. Practically every civilization which has conquered a vast empire has benefited from some new technology which gave them an advantage - an edge! We are all aware of the race for the atomic bomb between Germany and the Allies during World War II, and the race to develop planes and tanks which occurred during World War I. Less well known was the advance that gave the Mongols the ability to come out of nowhere and conquer most of the known world. They invented the stirrup, or were the first to improve upon it so that it allowed mounted cavalry to use their horses as a more effective fighting platform. Previously, cavalry often rode to battle and got off to fight. The Romans invented cement which they used to quickly build strong fortresses and the firm Roman roads to maintain their empire. The Hyksos exploded upon the scene with the battle chariot and swept over mighty Egypt. The Sea Peoples defeated the Hittites with swords and shields made of iron, harder than the bronze of their opponents.

The Hebrews brought a new technology to war, the *writing of God!* The written word played an important part in relaying commands, designing war machines, and training soldiers. This new technology of writing for war took some time to develop and utilize. **The effects of ideology, resulting from the written word, were immediate**! Armies had come into conflict for ages over territory and treasure. At least there was a kind of practical logic to this rationale for slaughter. With the onset of the word, men began to fight and die for ideas. **Ideological warfare was born!** The red-hot fervor and fanaticism of ideological warfare has not dimmed from that day to this one. There was a brutal face to it, as first displayed by Yehovah who directed that all idolaters be slain or driven out of the promised land so their abominations would perish with them. Those practices, like human sacrifice - needed to perish - nonetheless, pure ideological warfare takes no prisoners. Despite initial conquest, the Hebrews did not destroy their enemies and so their enemies returned to fight and conquer them.

Diaspora of the Hebrews

To illustrate the power of the writing of God as a technology, we must look at what it has done for the Israelites, or to them, over thousands of years. When the Israelites revolted against the Romans in 68 AD, their temple was destroyed. Those who were not killed or crucified were enslaved - exiled to every corner of the earth in a diaspora intended to rid the Romans of this stubborn people forever. **The writing of God was the glue which maintained Jewish cultural identity for almost two thousand years!**

Everywhere they lived Jewish children coming of age had to read the word and the writing of God from the Torah. Jewish people did not always assimilate well. Their peculiarities - kipas, ringlets, chanting and ancient religious scrolls written in a strange, mysterious tongue - made practitioners stand out. The tradition of literacy engendered by the writing of God often made the Jews more educated and successful than most members of the majority culture where they dwelt. They were persecuted, and often slaughtered, in untold numbers by periodic pogroms, anti-Jewish riots, which culminated in the great holocaust engineered by Hitler and the Nazis during World War II.

After the war, enormous numbers of Jews were displaced and living as refugees. Many emigrated to their ancestral homeland in Palestine. They rejoined the Jewish population that still existed there through the ages, creating the modern state of Israel. Since the immigrants spoke the languages of the myriad places they had lived for centuries, it made sense for Hebrew to be adopted as the common tongue of the new nation. This was an astonishing unparalleled phenomenon in the history of mankind! **Hebrew culture dispersed all over the globe for two thousand years retained enough cultural identity to come together again and form a nation!** The writing of God preserved a national identity through more time and trials than any other culture in history!

The persecution of the Jews is as acute today as it has ever been. Since the establishment of Israel, the Arab nations surrounding it have come to open war with Israel many times. Israel is surrounded by enemies whose hatred knows no bounds. Suicide bombings are a constant reminder of this ancient enmity. Arab news media regarding Israel or America are twisted to a ludicrous degree. Academic science is compromised. The author has lived, worked, and researched in Arab countries at various times and personally experienced the pressure on westerners to adopt the Arab perspective. Let it suffice to say anti-Semitism is alive and well!

Conclusions about the Writing of God

We have a message written by the finger of God in His own writing. **We find that *"writing of God"* (Thamudic) on the inscriptions at Mount Sinai in Midian!** Far from examining the medium for its importance, *the writing of God* has been ignored, assumed to be nothing more than a synonym for the message itself. This interpretation of *the writing of God* can no longer stand!

The scriptural evidence stated the writing of God was separate yet equally important to the word of God, not once but multiple times (Ex 24:12, Ex 34:27, Deut 6:8, Ex 32:16 *Amplified Bible*). In Revelation, which is heavily based upon Exodus, God stated, literally and figuratively, that He is the alphabet, *"I am Alpha and Omega, the first and the last: What you see, write in a book..."* (Rev 1:11). The Sinai Covenant was, and is, a teaching covenant for the purpose of reading and writing Scripture. The goal was to create a *"kingdom of Priests"* for the dissemination of the word and the writing of God to all the world, *"for all the world is mine"* (Ex 19:5-6). The covenant encompassed not only literacy and the word of God, but numeracy and mathematics.

History of the era makes it clear the Israelites were not a literate people before Sinai. They were slaves and nomads commanded to become a literate nation as their part in the Sinai Covenant. Moses was literate and knew the pictographic alphabet which was in limited use by Semites in the regions of Egypt, Sinai, Canaan, and Midian. It was Moses whom Yehovah used to teach the word and writing of God to the Levitical priesthood, who then taught the word and writing of God to the heads of families who were charged to *"teach them diligently"* unto their children.

Scripture was clear on the absolute prohibition against the making of graven images and the worship of idols or likenesses, even to the point of forbidding the dressing of monumental stone for writing, lest it lend it self to idolatry. Graven images refer specifically to the deified images of Egyptian hieroglyphs. The writing of God was not pictographic.

We know the Hebrew Torah is the oldest body of literature written in alphabetic script. We also know there has only been one alphabet from which all others derived. That alphabet appeared in the path of the Exodus at the time of the Exodus when Yehovah handed down the word and the writing of God to Moses on Mount Sinai. **Our primary conclusion is that the writing of God was the original alphabet of letter-symbols!**

Mount Sinai in Midian

The Bible states that Sinai was in Midian in Arabia. The historical record, according to Josephus, indicated Mount Sinai was the tallest mountain in Midian. Moses fled to Midian where he was married. He encountered Yehovah at the burning bush on Mount Horeb and was instructed to liberate the Israelites and bring them there to the mountain to worship God. The Sinai Peninsula was named upon the presumption that Mount Sinai was located there, a tradition that dates back to Queen Helena and the establishment of the Monastery of St. Catherine in the Sinai Peninsula. The traditional site was exhaustively searched and analyzed by the Israelis after the 1967 war and did not reveal any evidence of the events in Scripture proving it was the true site of the Mountain of God.

For example, there is no cave on the mountain. Scripture (1st Kings 19:8) states Elijah took refuge in a cave on Mount Horeb. Nor are any of the various other archaeological discoveries found at Sinai in Egypt. They are found at Sinai in Midian; inscriptions in the oldest alphabet known to linguistic science (Thamudic), columns to the 12 tribes, altar to the Golden Calf, footprints of the Israelites, altar to Yehovah for burnt offerings, and the split rock at Horeb. **Thus, the believer faces a decision to accept the location of Mount Sinai as church tradition decrees (in the Sinai Peninsula of Egypt) or as Scripture repeatedly states, in Midian in Arabia** (Gal 4:24). The historian must decide whether to give credence to the Bible as history, given this litany of facts and physical proof, or to leave it in the realm of legend.

Biblical Chronology

Historically, our discussion of events and problems of chronology indicated the biblical account offers a more reliable timeline. Events of the Old Testament are supported by evidence outside the Bible which tie them to the Exodus. For example, the Hittites were unknown outside of the Bible until the discovery of Hattusas, their capitol, in the 19th century. The Hyksos pharaohs are documented historically and indicated in the story of Joseph in Scripture. Numerous links to the pharaohs and events of the Exodus are found in Hittite and Egyptian records outside the Bible, such as the Amarna letters and the Papyrus of Ipuwer. The historical facts of the horrors and frequency of human sacrifice among pagan cultures made it evident why Yehovah condemned idolatry. The Anakim of the Bible (Josh 14:15), are also found in Greek myth. The giant Anak was killed when his kingdom of Anactoria in Turkey was conquered by the Capthorim-Philistim of the Bible.

These Capthorim-Philistim of Crete fought under Sarpedon to defend Troy. The trail of the giant *"sons of Anak"* (Num 13:13) leads us to the biblical Talmai (Num 13:22), or Thamúd of Arabia, whose name is attached to the most ancient alphabetic script, Thamudic, found at Mount Horeb in Midian.

The Yam Suph

The identification of *Yam Suph* as the *"Reed Sea"* is a faulty etymology brought on by a single translation of the word *suph* as papyrus in the Septuagint. The Yam Suph was given in Scripture as the southern boundary of Israel. Yam Suph meant *"Sea of Boundary"* to the Israelites and *"Sea of Edom"* to their neighbors, the Edomites. Yam Suph referred to the Gulf of Aqaba, an arm of the Red Sea, probably translated Red Sea because *edom* meant *red*.

We have identified two possible crossing sites, the Straits of Tiran and the Nuweiba Peninsula. Other stations of the Exodus, such as the bitter springs, the caves of Jethro, and the 12 springs of Elim are accounted for. At Rephidim, just 4 kilometers along a ridgeline from the summit of Mount Horeb, we find the Split Rock of Horeb, a geological wonder, split some 60 feet directly down the center with evidence of water erosion at its base.

The Footprints of the Israelites

Also, at Rephidim, we find we find footprints showing the Israelites did a ritual placing and tracing of the soles of the feet to claim their territory. **The footprints were marked with an alphabetic caption meaning the *"soles of the feet."*** The triple hash-mark, represented the letter K, was inscribed beside the soles of the feet. It was also used in a nearby alphabetic inscription, undeniable proof the triple hash-mark was used as a letter of the alphabet.

The Thamudic script used in the inscriptions at the base of Mount Sinai, and at Rephidim, is dated to the 15th century BC by experts at the Smithsonian and the Saudi Ministry of Antiquities. Proto-Semitic pictographs alongside of the inscriptions date them to the earliest era - during the transformation of alphabetic writing from pictographs to symbols. The 15th century BC was the period when the writing of God was given to Moses on Mount Sinai in Midian. These data establish a connection between the Proto-Semitic pictographs and the Thamudic alphabet, *"the writing of God,"* the father script of all alphabets.

At the base of Mount Sinai, we find two altars. The altar to the Golden Calf is covered with cattle worship motifs, three of which have a definite Egyptian origin. Two are replicas of the Apis bull ritual illustrated in the Serapeum at Memphis, the center of the Egyptian bull worship cult. The third depicts the suckling of Horus the cow goddess Hathor. This is why those sunk in idolatry said *"These be thy gods, O Israel"* (Ex 23:4) - in the plural, because the Golden Calf was surrounded by engraved sacred cattle worship motifs in typical Egyptian fashion. Other than the more primitive nature of the drawings, this is a fair approximation of how an altar site would have been sanctified in Egypt.

The second altar was that which Moses set up at the very base of the mountain to make burnt offerings to Yehovah. The Al-Bid Survey of Jabal l-Lawz did a preliminary dig of the altar site and discovered ash, organic remains and animal waste in the chamber at the end where the burnt offerings were made. The long narrow corrals of the altar site are unsuitable for human habitation but perfect for the queuing of animals to be slaughtered. Just beside the altar to Yehovah are the remains of the cut marble columns set up to the 12 tribes of Israel. The marble had to be quarried from a small vein at the top of the mountain and carried over torturous terrain to the base. It is a five-hour climb up the mountain.

The Inscriptions at Sinai

The Al-Bid Survey stated there was no evidence to date the stone (altar) structures at the base of the mountain. That would make their dating dependent upon the nearby inscriptions and petroglyphs. The inscriptions at Mount Sinai are mostly funerary, marking the place of death. These inscriptions included the name and the preface /zn/ meaning *deceased*. We have examined and translated four of these inscriptions. One used the triple hash-mark as a letter of the alphabet, "died *Kaliya*," thus validating our analysis of it as an alphabetic caption. Proto-Semitic pictographs were found beside the Kaliya inscription indicating a very early date. The second read *"died Amalek,"* recording the death of one of the soldiers of the Amalekites upon the Israelites (Ex 17:8). The Amalekites constantly preyed upon the weak and the stragglers (De 25:17-18). The third inscription included the name Hagar, a name associated with Mount Sinai in the Bible. **The fourth inscription was *"Amiah bat Hagar"* translated *"Amiah daughter of Hagar."* The use of the Hebrew word *"bat*," daughter, established these as Proto-Hebraic inscriptions!**

Ritual placing and tracing of footprints found near the Split Rock of Horeb at the area identified as Rephidim. Hash marks are an alphabetic caption for *"soles of feet"*.

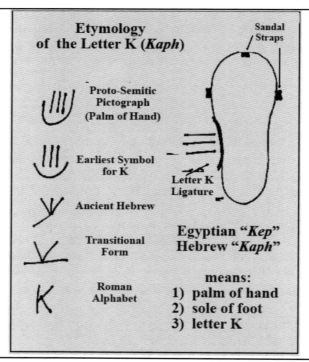

The letter K, a triple hash mark, was used beside the ritual placing and tracing of the feet at Rephidim, near Mount Sinai, to mean *soles of the feet*.
<u>This was the first literate act of the Israelites!</u>

Died Kaliya

Died Amalek

Thamudic inscriptions from Mount Sinai in Midian

<u>Above Left</u> - The inscription reads *Died Kaliya*
<u>Above Right</u> - The top line reads *Died Amalek*

<u>Bottom Left</u> - Top line reads *Died Hagar*
<u>Bottom Right</u> - *Died Amiah daughter of Hagar*

Died Hagar

Died Amiah daughter of Hagar

Photos reprinted by permission of Jim & Penny Caldwell
and the Split Rock Research Foundation.

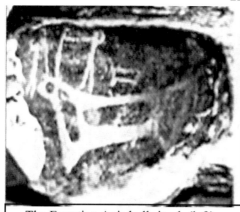 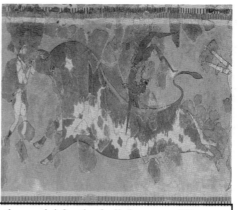

The Egyptian Apis bull ritual (left) was the model for the *bull dancers of Crete* (right), adopted into Iberian Spanish culture as the *bull fight*, imported to the Americas and developed into the rodeo *bull ride*. The photo (left) comes from Mt. Sinai in Arabia - the altar to the golden calf at Jabal al-Lawz. The image (right) comes from a fresco in Crete.

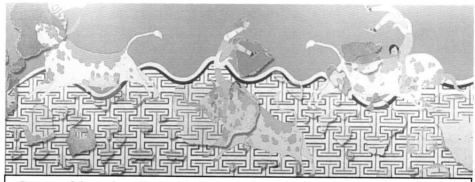

Images of the Apis Bull Ritual (above) are found in only four places in the world. Those (above) from Egypt at Avaris (start of the Exodus), also In Crete, Mycenae in Greece, and the bull worship imagery on the altars to the golden calf at Sinai.

Photos reprinted by permission of Dr. Sung Hak Kim.

Above & Right - Dr. Kim with a menorah inscribed in rock along the pilgrimage route to Mount Sinai, about 120 kilometers (75 miles) southeast. Various menorahs have been found among artifacts found in Arabia. It is an icon that dates directly from the historical events at Sinai. The inscription is in the south Thamudic alphabet circa 13th century BC.

Photos permission of Dr. Sung Hak Kim.

The name of God, YHVH, written back to front in ancient *Thamudic*, aka the *writing of God*, from Midian in Arabia. (circa 14th century BC)

The analysis of the research literature on the origin of the alphabet supports the assertion that the writing of God is the alphabet. The most recent evidence has destroyed the consensus of the Phoenician origin of the alphabet and pushed back the date by several centuries. The Semitic use of hieroglyphs as alphabetic pictographs may have begun as early as the 19th century BC. Examples of the Proto-Semitic pictographic alphabet have been found in Egypt, Sinai, Canaan and now on the inscriptions in Midian. Discovery of these characters at the Midian site is an important breakthrough linking these inscriptions at Mount Sinai with the changeover from an alphabet of pictographs to one of letters.

Path of the Exodus

The earliest discoveries of Proto-Semitic alphabetic characters show a clear progression in time and place along the path of the Exodus. The earliest alphabetic letter-symbols found in Midian are dated to the 15th century BC, followed by inscriptions found to the south in Sheba, then north in the Negev Desert, the south of Israel, then central Israel, and finally in northern Israel and southern Lebanon. The alphabet then spread to other points in the Mediterranean and eventually throughout the world.

These discoveries preclude the Phoenicians as the inventors of the alphabet. The credit given the Phoenicians was due to their monumental inscriptions. The Israelites were given an absolute prohibition against graven images and writing on dressed stone (Lev 26:1). That is why the stones of ancient Israel are mute.

The south Semitic inscriptions of Arabia were earlier than the north Semitic inscriptions of Byblos. While there are dozens of early inscriptions in the Canaan area, there are literally thousands in Arabia. Many are more ancient than those in Canaan, as early as 15th century BC, including the Thamudic inscriptions at Mount Horeb in Midian.

The Thamudic script of Midian is the earliest alphabetic script and the father script of both the north and south Semitic alphabets. Ten of the Thamudic letters show a clear derivation to both the Sabean alphabet to the south and the Paleo-Hebraic to the north. The ancient language expert Jacob Grimme claimed Thamudic was the original alphabet of letter-symbols as early as 1898. **In 1923, Grimme identified the Thamudic script as that of the Israelites of the Exodus!** In 1936, biblical archaeologist Stephen Caiger came to the same conclusion identifying the Thamudic script as the Minean-Sabean alphabet used by Moses at Sinai before the conquest of the promised land, during the wandering of the Israelites.

If Mount Sinai was in Midian in Arabia, then the commonly held belief that the Israelites wandered for forty years in the tiny Sinai Peninsula is incorrect. The revelations of the writing of God make it clear the Israelites were given the commission to spread the word and the writing of God. We see the earliest alphabetic inscriptions widely disseminated in Arabia. Given this new perspective, where the Israelites traveled during those forty years becomes a highly significant question.

An analysis of place names of the campsites in Exodus indicates the Israelites went south to Sheba. In Numbers 33 there are 18 consecutive sites we cannot identify except for two. One is Mount Sephar mentioned in Genesis as the boundary of the territory of the sons of Sheba, in south Arabia, and Dedan, in north Arabia. The second is Bene-Jaakan, a place name (Beni-Jookan) that still exists on the ancient border of Sheba in the Asir. It means sons of Jookan. In the Old Testament, Jooktan (or Jokshan) was the father of Sheba and Dedan. The name Beer-Sheba, meaning well of Sheba (or well of the Sabeans), was an indicator of the connection with the Sabeans who colonized the oases and wells of the north to control their lucrative caravan trade.

The discovery of the south Semitic inscriptions and votive stones in the area of Mount Horeb revealed that the mountain was a place of pilgrimage for centuries after the events of Sinai.

Thamudic inscriptions using a menorah have been found on the route to the mountain. Votive stones with menorahs and Thamudic inscriptions are fairly common. One such votive offering had a figurine of Moses with the word YHVH carved into the stone. These south Semitic inscriptions are evidence of pilgrims coming from Arabian, a highly significant find.

Implications of the Evidence

> My people are destroyed for lack of knowledge;
> Because you have rejected knowledge,
> I will also reject you, that you shall be no priest to me...
> (Hosea 4:6)

The writing of God guided believers to abandon superstition and take on the challenge of abstract, analytical thinking. This process has been credited almost entirely to the Greeks, not that we would want to dim their luster. Nonetheless, the western model of higher order thinking, no small event in the history of science, began with the Israelites and the writing of God. As more evidence continue to surface, it will require a serious re-orientation, if not a complete housecleaning, of biblical perspective of the era of the Exodus.

The Sinai Covenant changed the standard of writing from the use of graven images to the use of the alphabetic principle (one symbol - one sound) which made widespread literacy possible! These changes in the writing system moved mankind from concrete, referential thinking towards a capacity for abstract, rational thinking that would be described today as scientific thought. This new ideology precipitated what we have described as the great divide in human thought, the addition of analytical left-brained thinking in ideas to balance the right-brained holistic thinking in images.

It is, however, to the ideological battle that we must turn in illustrating the current relevance of the discoveries at Mount Sinai. The Sinai Covenant is the philosophical foundation of modern American democracy and education. That foundation is under attack. **The most important impact of the Sinai Covenant is on the education of our children! It was at Sinai where Yehovah gave us the word and the writing of God - His moral principle and His alphabetic principle.**

Chapter Three
Secularization of Education

My people are destroyed for lack of knowledge:
Because you have rejected knowledge,
I will also reject you, that you shall be no priest to me…
Hosea 4:6

The revelation that biblical scholars have ignored a major purpose of the Sinai Covenant, that which related to the writing of God, will hopefully stimulate a re-direction of biblical research and theological consideration. The role of Scripture in bringing literacy to mankind opens a critical new perspective. The writing of God guided believers to abandon superstition and take on the challenge of abstract, analytical thinking. This process has been credited almost entirely to the Greeks, not that we would wish to dim their luster. Nonetheless, the western model of higher order thinking, no small event in the history of science, began with the Israelites and the writing of God. As more evidence continues to surface, it will require a serious re-orientation, if not a complete housecleaning, of biblical perspective of the era.

The Sinai Covenant changed the standard of writing from the use of graven images to the use of the alphabetic principle. These changes in the writing system moved mankind from concrete, referential thinking towards a capacity for abstract, rational thinking that would be described today as the beginnings of scientific thought. This new ideology precipitated what the author has described as *'the great divide in human thought,'* the addition of analytical left-brained thinking in ideas to balance the right-brained holistic thinking in images.

The word and the writing of God guided believers to a deeper spiritual comprehension, commitment and communion with their Creator. In every age believers have struggled with the conflict between spiritual and earthly desires. It is an old story, as relevant today as when Moses descended the mountain with the tablets of the Ten Commandments. Tracing the development of this ideology throughout history is far beyond the scope of this book. It is, however, to the ideological battle that we must turn in illustrating the current relevance of the discoveries at Mount Sinai. The Sinai Covenant is the philosophical foundation of modern American democracy and education. **That foundation is under attack. The most important impact of the Sinai Covenant is on the education of our children!**

In America, the movement is afoot to secularize the public square. Despite the fact this country was established as a haven for religious freedom, the concept of separation of church and state has been turned against religion. The First Amendment to the United States Constitution states that *"Congress shall make no law respecting an establishment of religion, or prohibiting the free exercise thereof..."* The phrase *"separation of church and state"* was a later interpretation of the First Amendment, not a part of the U.S. Constitution.

Those who do not trust the moral code of God - seek to eliminate religious ideas from our founding documents and system of laws. The First Amendment has therefore been re-interpreted by some to mean that any mention of God in a public place, or document, should be considered promoting a state religion. Therefore, they attempt to have the words, *"under God"* thrown out of the Pledge of Allegiance or *"In God we trust"* erased from our coinage.

That perspective completely ignores the second part of the First Amendment - not to prohibit the free exercise of religion. If we can no longer acknowledge that our country was founded to allow us to freely worship God - is that not quashing the free exercise of religion? Should we sterilize all our founding documents and remove any mention of God so those who are uncomfortable with religion will feel better?

All these issues are part and parcel of the continuing debate sparked by the Sinai Covenant. The Sinai Covenant was the opening salvo in an ideological struggle never before seen and which has never ceased. In the ancient world, when a conqueror took territory he might pull down the statues to the old gods and establish new ones, but that was not the purpose of conquest. Conquest was about territory, religion was of little import.

The Israelites conquest of the promised land was about religion - territory was secondary. The purpose of the invasion was to establish a nation to the one true God and to drive out or destroy idolaters so their abominations, such as human sacrifice, would die with them. **God's moral principle anchored freedom so that no politician or tyrant can claim authority to take them away!** We must not lose track of the all-important historical clash of ideas amidst the clash of arms. The real conquest took place in the hearts and minds of Yehovah's chosen people.

The real conquest was ideological. It was a call for the chosen people to submit themselves to the Covenant of Yehovah. It was a call to educate themselves in the word and writing of God. It was a call to a new more rigorous way of thinking - to develop abstract, analytical, rational thought. It was a call to read, write, calculate, and create a cultural model to serve as the prototype of civilization!

The front lines of this culture war are in the classroom. The progressive education approach was created by secular humanists like John Dewey. The Humanist Manifesto, authored by Dewey, outlined a radical social agenda that is now being foisted upon American schoolchildren daily. The key concepts of that agenda are radical secularism. The approaches to education that engender that agenda need to be exposed and debated. Their disastrous effect on literacy and education in general are a matter of fact. The analysis of these deeply flawed methodologies account for the crisis in education - scandals of cheating and drop-out rates - already occurring all over the country. In addition, they point to the coming crisis of civil war in our nation as a result of this radicalized education system and the graduates it produces. These failures are traced to the rejection of the moral principle, and the alphabetic principle, handed down from Mount Sinai.

The Logical End of Secularism

The founding fathers sought to avoid the precepts of any particular religious denomination being mandated upon the nation as a whole. They never dreamed their words would be used to eliminate God from public discourse! There is a fallacy in the separation of church and state as presently promoted. When carried to its logical conclusion no one overtly practicing religion is considered fit to serve the public interest. Therefore, only those who efface their Judeo-Christian beliefs, or nave none, are fit to serve in government. This creates a government that is strongly anti-religious. We see this now in a highly secularized school system.

Those who advocate this secularization of America should pause to reconsider. **The basic premise of our Declaration of Independence was that humans are *"endowed by their Creator with certain unalienable rights"* not subject to approval or removal by human authority.** Once God is successfully eliminated as the ultimate authority for our rights, then by what authority are they given? They will be interpreted and guaranteed by the authority of the state, who will re-interpret those rights, or dismiss them, according to the latest doctrine of political correctness.

The state can end up totalitarian! The constitution of the Soviet Union rang with the same stirring rhetoric about rights as the U.S. Constitution but the reality was brutal oppression. To those who do not like that our rights are *"endowed by our Creator,"* just wait until our rights are ordained by government. For the state giveth and the state taketh away. According to our founding fathers, the basis of freedom in America is that our God-given rights are above the authority of the state because government can never be completely trusted.

The author is reminded of two recent court decisions rendered the same week. A lower court ruled that a student accused of cursing his teacher was exercising his right to freedom of speech. The second decision was to remove the monument to the Ten Commandments from the lobby of the Alabama Supreme Court building. The U.S. Supreme Court banned school-sponsored prayer in the public schools in 1962. That decision is still expanding in its interpretation such as the decision to remove the Ten Commandments. In the modern world of political correctness, there can be little censure except, it seems, when it comes to separating church and state. **Once we depart from a God-given moral code, we may well end up in a world of human biases where praying to God in school is forbidden but cursing one's teacher is protected as a constitutional right to freedom of speech!**

God as Moral Authority

In antiquity, respect for the gods was based more on fear of their power than their grasp of truth. All calamity or good fortune was attributed to the power of the gods. The actions of the gods as they come down to us in myth show a caprice as immature as that of a spoiled child. The gods were thought to have divine attributes - some were considered all-seeing, all-knowing, and all-powerful - but most were the less-than-perfect scion of an equally flawed host of other gods and godlets. This celestial soap opera bred superstition and entrapped believers in a straightjacket of ignorance and impotency. All outcomes were decided by the whim of the gods. This belief bred fatalism in its adherents and prevented them from understanding the natural laws of the universe. The gods were never a moral authority. Yehovah proclaimed them to be false gods, idols of stone and nothing more! The way of Yehovah was to give wings to believers via spiritual faith to sustain and support them and education to enlarge and enlighten them. The challenge was to abandon the snare of superstition and accept a moral authority and purpose higher than that of humanity. That was the ideal of the Sinai Covenant!

Secularization of the Classroom

The Sinai Covenant was, and is, an education covenant. The alphabet, as well as the alphabetic principle, were handed down from Mount Sinai. We know Yehovah did not want the letter-symbols of the alphabet to become sacred symbols lest they be idolized and worshiped, defeating the purpose of their creation. The Sinai Covenant has current and crucial relevance to us all. If this were not so the author would now conclude the academic arguments on ancient scripts and the origin of the alphabet and leave it as that. For readers whose interest is biblical knowledge of the ancient world, well... their task is finished. **For those who wish to know the power of the writing of God in the education of our children today, that quest has just begun!**

Above all, the Sinai Covenant is a call for believers to take diligent responsibility for their children's education. This is where the moral battle takes its most important stand. The transformation of the public schools is the central objective of the campaign to secularize America. That struggle takes place in the methods and materials used to educate America's children. It is there, out of sight of everyone but education experts, where the battle for America's children is being won or lost. The tenets of secular humanism have been steadily implemented and expanded in the public schools via progressive education which has demonstrably degraded academic achievement, student behavior, and moral values. The two central causes of this debacle are the rejection of the moral and the alphabetic principles of God given at Sinai.

The alphabetic principle, in its purest form, is one symbol - one sound. Each sound of the language is represented by a symbol allowing anyone to achieve literacy. By using the alphabetic principle, whatever one's alphabet happens to be, the learner will practice sounding out the letters to recognize the words.

Phonics is the process of using the alphabetic principle to learn the sound-symbol correspondences, rules, and sounding out that enable children to read easily and well. Early systematic phonics is a relatively simple process which works rapidly and reliably with almost all children. Literacy is the lynchpin of the entire educational system and if that single skill is not mastered then all else is lost. We will examine how the suppression of the alphabetic principle in our school system is making us a nation of illiterates. **The Sinai Covenant is about the alphabetic principle as surely as it is about the moral principle of God.**

John Dewey

It is not simply literacy that is affected. The precepts of progressive education have degraded the moral principle of schooling. At the turn of the 20th century, progressive education was championed by John Dewey. Dewey began teaching at the University of Chicago in 1894 under the mentorship of Colonel Francis Parker, whom Dewey called the *"father of progressive education."* By the time of Parker's death in 1902, Dewey had become the undisputed philosophical leader of the progressive education movement. John Dewey is not to be confused with Milton Dewey, the designer of the Dewey Decimal System. John Dewey's legacy was training several generations of teachers from the prestigious University of Chicago School of Education. He proposed nothing less than a blueprint for the complete restructuring of American public schools. The progressive education movement has gained ground steadily throughout the past century. Today, progressive education has a lock on public education! Although future teachers enter modern teacher education colleges with the same attitudes toward academic achievement as most Americans, they come out of college with 95% identifying themselves as progressive educators. How did this come about?

Jean Jacques Rousseau was one of the philosophical founders of this movement. During the 18th century, he rhapsodized that the ideal of education was to be in harmony with natural perfection. This concept of romantic naturalism was based on Rousseau's development of a fictional character he called Emile. Rousseau described Emile's *"ideal"* natural education and the beneficial results thereof. Rousseau argued that all God had created in nature was good - substituting a doctrine of original goodness for original sin. As such, formal schooling was considered not only unnecessary but harmful to students by perverting their natural tendencies. These concepts were adopted into progressive education and are impacting the education of children today more than ever before. For example, the dominant modern theory of literacy states that reading, like speaking, is a natural process and the teacher's best practice is to simply allow spontaneous natural development by presenting *"authentic"* learning experiences. In practice, this means that teachers do little more than read to the children and push extremely simple, repetitive, illustrated books at them, hoping they will crack the phonetic code subconsciously. The progressive education approach to literacy has a long record of disastrous failure because it ignores **the self-evident reality that reading is not natural, it is cultural! Children do not learn to read spontaneously as they learn to talk. They must be taught to read!**

Secular Humanism & Progressive Education

Progressive education is part of a philosophy called secular humanism. We will examine its history, key concepts, and the academic and behavioral results of implementing progressive education in America's schools. These concepts are in distinct opposition to the precepts handed down from Mount Sinai which established a higher power as the source of ultimate truth and wisdom. Humanism worships humanity and eliminates God. Such a philosophy violates the First Commandment *"You shall have no other gods before me"* (Ex 20:3). The pursuit of this philosophy has thrown modern education into chaos. Public education has become entangled in practices that are increasingly ludicrous, even to the lay observer. The results of those practices are catastrophic, yet the juggernaut of progressive education continues unchecked. The actions of the originator speak for their beliefs. Once we see clearly what they believed, we will be prepared to witness the results of replacing God's philosophy with a humanist one.

Humanism has been institutionalized in the American school system under the rubric of progressive education. It sanctifies natural learning which, in practice, marginalizes the role of the only person in the classroom who actually knows the subject, the teacher. In this theory all learning, all truth, is individually constructed, therefore external standards need not apply. A child's constructed comprehension of a subject is considered more significant than an expert's mastery. The teacher's role is as a facilitator, not as someone with superior knowledge. This shift of authority from external sources to an internal source not only eliminates God as a teacher but also replaces Him as the source of ultimate truth. **All answers are found within the human nature. Humanity has triumphed! God is dead!**

Look-Say Method for the Deaf

The Look-Say Method was first developed by Thomas Gallaudet for teaching deaf children. **The Look-Say Method dropped phonics from the teaching of literacy.** Since the deaf do not know the sounds of English, phonics need play little part in teaching children, deaf from birth, to read. In 1836, the Boston Primary School Committee, as part of reforms advocated by Horace Mann, decided to try Gallaudet's primer on an experimental basis. IN 1839, Horace Mann and his fellow reformers established the first state-owned teacher training college, the Normal School at Lexington, Massachusetts.

The reformers seem to have forgotten one supremely important factor. The vast majority of schoolchildren are not deaf. *"In the very first year of the very first state teachers college in America, the look-say method of teaching reading was taught to its students as the preferred and superior method of literacy"* (Koeltzow, 2000:p.2). By 1844, a group of Boston schoolmasters published an article thoroughly critiquing and condemning the look-say method as inefficient in most cases and totally disastrous in others. Progressive educators were not deterred. By 1881, the publishers of the McGuffey Readers were lauding the new *"Sight Word Method,"* based on Look-Say, as an alternative to phonics.

John Dewey - New Patriarch of Progressive Education

The progressive education movement found a leader to replace Horace Mann when Colonel Francis Parker became superintendent of public schools in Quincy, Massachusetts. Later, from 1899-1901, he was head of the University of Chicago School of Education. It was there that Parker mentored John Dewey. Dewey created a Laboratory School for children at the University of Chicago. Students were taught by the Look-Say Method. Dewey's book, *School and Society*, catapulted him to the leadership of the progressive movement upon Parker's death. Dewey's goals were social more than educational. This was expressed by his theme of *"Living is primary, learning is secondary"* and his pedagogic creed, *"I believe that education is the fundamental method of social progress and reform."* In his creed Dewey invoked God saying that a teacher who followed Dewey's methods was *"a prophet of the true God"* because Dewey's approach was sure to usher in *"the true kingdom of God."* Although Dewey's philosophy was atheistic, he seems to have had few qualms about using religiosity to promote his ideas.

John Dewey was the principal author of *The Humanist Manifesto*, first published in 1933. The Manifesto dispensed with God and espoused the idea that humanity is inherently good and that scientific man, through innovation, can resolve all the problems of the world. In the early part of the 20th century, America was enduring the excesses of the robber barons, their employees worked long hours at little pay. Although their excesses were not the norm, many intellectuals during the era of the 1920s and 30s seized on communism and it atheistic doctrine as the hope of the future. **Dewey was, to use a common expression, a card-carrying Communist.** Communists, like Dewey and many other humanists, certainly planned for it to be established in the U.S. John Dewey was a rising star in world communist circles.

The Humanist Manifesto

One of the most notable of Bolshevik educators, Albert Pinkevitch regarded Dewey as the foreign thinker closest to the spirit of Marxism and Russian Communism. Dewey's ideas were popularized in Russia after the Bolshevik Revolution of 1917. It seemed a natural fit at the time since Dewey's ideas were certainly revolutionary. When Dewey visited Russia in 1928 as member of a delegation of American communists, he professed his amazement *"at the progress already made"* in the Soviet school system, which he described as *"a going concern, a self-moving organism!"* Dewey wrote of his Russian experiences in the essay published in 12929, *"Impressions of Soviet Russia and the Revolutionary World."*

In the late 1930s Leon Trotsky, one of the originators of Communism, was exiled from Russia by the Soviet Politburo in a power struggle initiated by Stalin. Dewey traveled to Mexico City to meet with Trotsky. Dewey organized and chaired the Trotsky Inquiry, which was published under his name in 1938 as *"The Case of Leon Trotsky."* Dewey declared Trotsky *"not guilty"* of the Politburo's charges!

This led to the condemnation of Dewey in the communist world where he had enjoyed international prominence. Stalin eliminated Dewey's methods from Soviet schools. Dewey became the principal author of *The Humanist Manifesto* in 1933, which nonetheless incorporated the goals of international Socialism, the tamer brand of Communism.

The Humanist Manifesto Decrees

1) Religious humanists regard the universe as self-existing, not created.
2) The nature of the universe depicted by modern science makes unacceptable any supernatural or cosmic guarantees of human values.
3) Humanism considers the complete realization of human personality the end goal of life and seeks its fulfillment in the here and now.
4) It follows that there will be no uniquely religious emotions and attitudes of the kind hitherto associated with belief in the supernatural.
5) Religious institutions, their ritualistic forms, ecclesiastical methods, and communal activities must be reconstituted...
6) Humanists are firmly convinced that existing acquisitive and profit-motivated society has shown itself to be inadequate and that a radical change ...a socialized and cooperative economic order must be established to the end that the equitable distribution of the means of life be possible ...**Humanists demand a shared life in a shared world!**

Humanist Manifesto II

In 1973 the Humanist Movement published these clarifications:

1) Salvationism, based on mere affirmation, still appears as harmful, diverting people with false hope of heaven hereafter. Reasonable minds look to other means for survival.
2) **The next century can and should be the humanist century!**
3) Humanity, to survive, requires bold and daring measures. Only a shared world and global measures will suffice.
4) Humanism can provide the purpose and inspiration that so any seek - giving personal meaning and significance to human life.
5) Many kinds of humanism exist in the contemporary world. The varieties and emphases of naturalistic humanism include, *"scientific," "ethical," "democratic," "religious,"* and *"Marxist"* humanism. *"...Free thought, atheism, agnosticism, skepticism, deism, rationalism, ethical culture, and liberal religion"* all claim to be heir to the humanist tradition.
6) We find insufficient evidence for belief in the... supernatural.
7) As non-theists we begin with humans not God, nature not deity.
8) Promises of immortal salvation ...distract humans from present concerns, from self-actualization...
9) There is no real evidence life survives the death of the body.
10) Religions are not the only obstacles to human progress.
11) Ethics is ...situational, needing no theological sanction.
12) The right to birth control, abortion, and divorce are recognized.
13) Individuals should be permitted to express their sexual proclivities and pursue their life-styles as they desire.
14) Recognition of an individual's right to die with dignity, euthanasia, and the right to suicide.
15) The schools should foster satisfying and productive living.
16) Innovative, experimental forms of education are welcomed.

The humanism brought into being by Dewey is precisely reflected in the goals and methods of progressive education. The Humanist Manifesto of 1973 serves to illustrate that those policies have not changed, merely deepened. Anyone studying the decline of educational achievement in the public schools can see the fruition of this philosophy and the damage it has done. I have wondered many times during my career whether I can openly express my Christian values and still be accepted by academia as a serious scientist! The very fact that I have to ask that question is a sign of the predominance of the secular humanist philosophy in modern education and science.

Key Educational Concepts

John Dewey was the originator of many concepts and terms embedded in modern education. Many of his theories were discredited by extensive experimental research as early as the 1950s. Nonetheless, they persist as the basis of modern academic theory under various names such as Constructivism, Developmentalism, Whole Language, and Whole Math. Some of the key concepts are reflective thinking, hands-on experience, authentic learning, authentic assessment, child-centered education, and the '*whole child.*' Progressive education states that the child possesses a natural developmental sequence in learning and those learning experiences that imitate this natural development are superior. Anything that interferes with these natural choices by the student is deemed harmful. For example, student interest is the sole legitimate rationale for any educational effort. Students should not be expected to work at anything they are not interested in. This kind of thinking turns modern education into a dog-and-pony show where teachers are supposed to entertain students to motivate them rather than hold them to a set of standards. As a result of this concept of *natural perfection*, teachers and parents are often discouraged from interfering with their children's natural development.

This idealism in education probably arose as a reaction to harsh teaching methods of an earlier era, such as the Prussian military model of education. In some European countries, such as Germany, teachers of the 1800s were often retired drill sergeants and their discipline was adapted from military training methods. By contrast, **the Laboratory School for children set up by Dewey at the University of Chicago either enraptured visitors or horrified them!** Those who believed in the underlying goodness of taking a natural approach to learning found refreshment and inspiration in the lack of structure. **There was no curriculum - no proscribed course of study. Those who were of a more practical mindset and expected children to read, write, and calculate as a result of their schooling, were sadly disappointed!**

Authentic Learning Experience

Having thrown out the books in pursuit of authentic learning experiences, progressive educators came up with authentic assessment to judge their learning outcomes. Authentic assessment survives today in the guise of *portfolio assessment.* Instead of standardized testing, a teacher collects samples of student work in a portfolio to illustrate their progress, or lack of it.

Judging achievement via portfolio assessment can be very subjective and ambiguous. Comparison of individuals or groups of students to a norm is impossible. Accountability is the first casualty of authentic assessment. This method of teaching prompted the fad of Outcome-Based Education in the 1980s which died out rapidly when it was widely recognized that there were few outcomes and little education upon which to base any kind of assessment.

Progressive education sanctifies the proclivities of the student as superior to any that might be imposed upon them. As a university professor responsible for supervising student teachers implementing such naturalistic methods, the author was a firsthand witness to the results. I did not participate in establishing the program nor teaching it. I was solely responsible for judging whether the student teachers were doing it correctly as they were trained.

I remember distinctly one student teacher was doing a research project with her fifth graders concerning the Battle of Puebla, where the untrained and poorly armed Mexican peasants defeated a French army of professional soldiers. The teacher was to elicit the students' prior knowledge relating to the topic and let them determine what areas of research they wanted to pursue. The teacher implemented the technique correctly. After a brief presentation of the battle, the teacher opened the discussion of research to a thundering silence. The teacher was not allowed to provide, or even suggest, avenues since that was deemed likely to dampen the students' natural curiosity. As Dewey would say, ***"We shall not dig a channel for the student's river of curiosity but rather let it find its own natural course!"***

The students' *"river of curiosity"* was suffering from a severe drought on that particular day. The students sat bored and disinterested. They knew if they responded it meant they would have to do research work and if they did not respond then they might not have to do anything. Finally, after sufficient prodding, a student asked *"Did they have gangs back then?"* This became the students' research topic for the Battle of Puebla. Not only is the topic irrelevant but also - fifth graders are not equipped to research the *gang issue* as it relates to the Battle of Puebla. They learned little to nothing from this *tour de farce* of naturalistic education.

Dewey's approach was to put children into problem-solving situations which required them to utilize reflective thinking. The idea of reflective thinking is that a student has to use his innate capacities rather than rote learning to solve a problem.

Reflective thinking presumably encourages a child to more creative output - thinking outside the box. This puts enormous pressure on the teacher to come up with appropriate, *authentic* problem-solving situations which successfully challenge each student. If the student fails to rise to the occasion, according to the theory, the blame falls on the teacher who failed to successfully engage the natural proclivity to learn. Repeated failure on the part of the student is excused. The student was simply not developmentally ready to succeed at that moment and if given time would become ready naturally. Forcing them to learn too early is *"not developmentally appropriate"* and could cause serious harm to the student. **For example, practice of basic skills such as sounding-out words or addition and subtraction, is considered monotonous and demotivating to students. Progressive education emphasizes problem solving rather than mastery of skills.**

Higher Order Thinking vs Basic Skills

In reality, higher-order problem solving is at the peak of a pyramid whose foundation is mastery of basic skills. The author, having spent a lifetime in education, has seen all of the progressive education methods is use. Almost all of the examples given are from firsthand experience. In the author's home state of Texas, probability and statistics, algebraic thinking, and geometric formulation are all part of the curriculum. As early as kindergarten they are implemented for children who cannot yet count to ten. What, you might ask can you teach a child about probability and statistics before they can count? Well, you can flip a coin and explain that it comes up heads half the time and tails half the time - presuming the child understands *heads*, *tails*, and *half*. It is estimated students need only 7-9 minutes of practice daily to master math operations. The evaluation of standardized test results reveal that many, if not most, students do not get even that small amount of practice in a seven-hour school day. The author has personally witnessed the lack of basic skills practice in the public schools and can attest to the truth of that conclusion.

Constructivism

Reflective thinking is an individual way of grasping knowledge but, as it is different for each student, we are told that it cannot be taught. This way of thinking spawned numerous educational practices such as Constructivism, and Discovery Learning. The basis of Constructivism is that learners *construct* knowledge from the input around them and that '*construct*' is effective in comprehending the world. It is also preferable to anything that might have been proscribed for them.

The premise of Constructivism is that a child's natural innate capacities are superior to skills taught by experienced teachers. According to Dewey, the information garnered incidental to the education process is the only type we should consider important. In other words, whatever children get out of the process is what matters, not what they should get. According to progressive educators, all meaning is individual, therefore, old paradigms are practically meaningless and students can just as well invent their own paradigms. **One might note that taking this to its logical end would eliminate all standards of learning - which is indeed the direction of modern education.** The resistance from educators to standards and standardized testing is intense.

The Socratic Method - Discovery Learning

This Constructivist ideal has been formalized in a method known as the Discovery Method or Socratic Method. Socrates once led a student to an understanding of some basic geometric concepts without ever telling him the answers. When used sparingly, this can sometimes be an effective technique. However, it is typically applied as a one-trick-pony to all problems at all levels of education from elementary to university. Progressive education might better be described as regressive education. It advocates that students reinvent the wheel and every innovation in every subject that took, the most brilliant minds, millennia to polish and perfect. Students should not have to reinvent the whole of mathematical thought - from fractions to astrophysics - without ever knowing if their efforts are correct or not!

The effects of these methods are damaging students at all levels. In one literacy training video, teachers were to put new words on a *word wall*. Since they were to let student spelling of these words develop naturally, teachers put the students' *"inventive"* (meaning *"incorrect"*) spelling up on the word wall without comment or correction.

Progressive educators see it as more beneficial to applaud a student's effort by enshrining incorrect spelling attempts than to risk damaging a sensitive ego and newfound curiosity by correcting errors. **It is assumed students' inventive spelling will gradually self-correct as they read and write more. In my experience, it seldom does.** Spelling has been one of the notable defects of progressive education. These practices show a system-wide willingness to apply inept innovation on a colossal scale without controlled studies testing for its efficacy first. Two examples should serve to clarify the wide-spread disaster of the Socratic Method, aka Discovery Learning, in the classroom.

I was teaching sixth grade mathematics at a Learning Center in Dallas, Texas, where the latest innovations were being used. One day, two special consultants were sent into my classroom to teach using the Socratic Method. The subject was powers. They used a notational formula that was different from what is normally used. For example, for the problem of 5 x 5 written as 5^2 these consulting experts would write 5E2, meaning *Five-Exponent-Two*. They spent an hour with my sixth graders trying to teach the basic concepts of powers. I was only to observe so I said nothing.

The two special consultants failed completely. The sixth graders never figured out what they were doing and, of course, the consultants never told them. When they had left I told my students they were teaching powers and the lights went on in their eyes instantly. I had already taught them powers and roots. They were reasonably proficient at these kind of calculations but never grasped that the consultants were presenting it in a variant type of notation. **So, the Discovery Method failed dramatically to *teach* them something they already knew very well!**

The second example took place in my daughter's physics program at a well-respected university. I was able to sit in on several of her physics classes. It was painful to watch every time. The students struggled to grasp what the teacher was trying to get across, without ever telling them the correct answers, of course. These were good students, the best our high schools had to offer. The students, including my daughter, were spending insane amounts of time trying to teach themselves the physics they were not getting taught in the classroom. They were getting tutors, spending 20-30 hours a week or more studying this one subject. **They were trying as hard as they could, breaking their hearts against the insanity of Discovery Learning!** For those who lasted into the higher level physics classes the professors were steamed that the students just did not know the basics that were "*covered*" in previous classes. One by one, they dropped out of the physics program. **The entire Physics Department graduated only *one* student per year!**

Obviously, this was deeply troubling to me since I had convinced my daughter to go into science rather than one of the playdough majors. She changed her major to Spanish which required her to do an extra year of college. Her comment when we discussed it was that even if she did manage to graduate as a physics major - **she hated physics so much she was never going to work in the field of mathematics!** This was the result with the best of our students. You can imagine the result with the others.

Right-Brainers vs Left-Brainers

Progressive education theory exalts right-brain over left-brain processing. It does not take long to realize this one-way street is seriously misguided. Right-brainers demonize left-brain skills such as phonics and mastery of math operations. Higher order thinking skills (HOTS) are not an entirely right-brain process. They require learners to tackle a practical problem, synthesize all they know, and restructure the problem in a way that it can be solved. At the base of the HOTS pyramid are left-brain skills. The taller the pyramid of higher order thinking, the broader must be the base of foundational basic skills. No base - no pyramid!

Both left-brained logical, analytical thinking and right-brain wholistic thinking are distinctly different but essential to effective brain function. The proper mix of left-brain vs right-brain approaches in education is both a science and an art. It is not a balance that is called for but a matching of the right tools to the task - how many parts analysis to how many parts synthesis. Progressive education promotes right-brain wholistic problem solving before basic skills even in elementary school. Children are often asked to write before they can read, to solve math word problems before they have mastered math operations. Progressive educators promote the use of calculators to replace *rote* learning. They promote reading to children instead of children reading via phonics.

Progressive educators promote a reading methodology which is almost completely right-brained (*"You learn to read by reading!"*). Their challengers maintain beginning readers need left-brained practice of isolated skills (phonics & sounding-out words). It is much like two carpenters arguing over whether to build a house with a hammer or a saw while the house under construction is falling apart. The most often-mentioned solution is to achieve a balance of the two processes. I suggest that it is wiser to approach it as a master carpenter. One does not build a house by using the saw half the time and the hammer half the time. The master recognizes the value of both tools and uses the tool needed for the task.

Most multiple choice tests are left-brained because an exam typically requires knowledge of precise facts and manipulation of the knowledge using basic operations that must be learned and practiced. A right-brain wholistic type of exam would be an essay test where there are numerous ways to express an answer. Although this is a valid and important means of testing, sometimes the grading of essays can be annoyingly subjective. One teacher's A paper is another teacher's C paper.

Standardized exams do not contain this kind of bias - they must be comparable. Right-brainers dismiss left-brained basic skills testing. For example, standardized testing, heavily dependent upon mastery of basic skills, is often condemned by progressive educators. The chorus of complaints usually claim left-brain exams do not test what is really important, that is, the right-brain skills they supposedly teach. When pinned on the question of precisely which skills are really important, *creativity* usually heads the list. Progressive educators typically dismiss and ignore all objective test results showing their methods to be a failure. Billions of taxpayer dollars and millions of children's futures are routinely gambled upon the latest untested right-brain fad rather than research-based methods and materials proven to work.

Developmentalism

Classroom instruction under progressive education has shifted from the product to the process. One variety of progressive education is called Developmentalism. All teaching must adapt to students' individual developmental sequence in order to facilitate their intrinsic motivation. To expect too little, we are told, is a healthier way to approach the child's development than to expect too much. The National Education Association (NEA), the largest teachers' union, is one of the primary endorsers of this approach:

> We need to look more at the process and performance of our students and less at the more narrow and self-defeating emphasis of product or acquisition. If a student is responding with enthusiasm and interest, she/he will probably learn, but often without a neat, continuous, daily progress line. To lose our students' excitement and involvement for lack of immediate learning is not only a waste of effort but also a danger to the ultimate goal of any teacher - a student who is on the road to becoming a lifelong learner.
> (NEA Journal by Wodkowski, 1986:p.16)

The unquestioned assumption is that students will become internally motivated to study if we approach them correctly! In other words, do not require that they produce. That might be demoralizing. Entice them to produce at their own pace, or leisure, and they will ultimately be more motivated, as measured over a lifetime rather than by end-of-year exams. The technique espoused is to await the *"teachable moment"* when the student questions something, perhaps a point of grammar like the use of subjective tense. At that moment the student is open!

That is the *"teachable moment!"* At that moment the questioning student is open to absorbing the presentation of information on that topic. This puts insufferable demands upon the teacher. It is common for teachers to have 100 objectives to cover with their 20 students over a week's time. **This will require 2000 individual *teachable moments* - few of these will ever come.** Even an eager, motivated student does not know what questions to ask. In the absence of motivated students, quite the norm in many classrooms - **Developmentalism leads to a disabling hesitancy on the part of teachers to require mature and responsible behavior on the part of their students even in the face of clear deficiencies of knowledge and problematic conduct!**

Developmentally appropriate practices are the spearhead of progressive education today. It is so well-entrenched in public education that is is considered conventional wisdom. Developmentalism tolerates bad behavior, immaturity, and poor performance. It presumes that positive character traits inevitably emerge if the child is properly facilitated. However, attempts to directly demand, expect or induce positive behavior are usually deemed *not* developmentally appropriate.

> Schools [are encouraged] to spare neither effort nor resources in fitting instruction to students while expecting little from them in return. Student inattention and apathy are meet with Herculean efforts to stimulate interest and enthusiasm. Deficient outcomes are countered by reducing expectations to the level of whatever the student seems willing to do... recurrent failure to attain even minimal achievement is accepted as lamentable but unavoidable... **In short, developmentalism requires only the teacher to work, not the student!** (Stone, 1994:p.62)

We need to understand why our children are rioting in the streets today. Students taught this way have weak minds. They are not critical thinkers - capable of logical analysis and argumentation. **Note that professors do not use any of these bogus methods when preaching political indoctrination.** They straight-out tell their students what they should believe. Students know little history - not even the basic logical premise that there are two sides to every story. Professors often belittle or punish those who have another viewpoint than their own. I long ago learned that to stand up to a teacher who was teaching dubious methods, materials, or facts - would most likely cost you a letter grade. We need to grade students fairly but **we need to grade our educational methods and materials as well!**

This Research-Based Scale was created by the author to guide assessment of methods and materials. Start in the middle at **the 50 score mark - those methods or materials have not been tested, or provided inconclusive results.** There are many things that could cause testing to not be effective. There was no homogeneity of the experimental group. There was no control group. The tests used may have been poorly designed.

RESEARCH - BASED METHODS SCALE

Miles R Jones
Texas A & M - Commerce

100 Super scale testing with replication, longitudinal & demographic data

90 Large scale field testing (1000+ Ss) with more than one replication

80 Medium scale field testing (100+ Ss) w' replication [**positive** results]

70 Small scale field testing (-100 Ss) [**positive** comparative **results**]

60 Significant corroborating evidence **supporting** methodology

50 *Contradictory or insignificant corroborating evidence*

40 Significant corroborating evidence **contra-indicating** methodology

30 Small scale field testing (-100 Ss) [**negative** comparative **results**]

20 Medium scale field testing (100+ Ss) w' replication [**neg. results**]

10 Large scale field testing (1000+ Ss) with more than one replication

0 Super scale testing with replication, longitudinal & demographic data

*<u>**All methods below 50 failed!**</u> <u>They had negative results!</u>

* All hard data must be based on comparative results with widely used benchmark instruments such as ITBS, SAT, TAAS, NAEP etc.

Corroborating evidence means research other than testing.

Any score higher than 50 comes from <u>positive results</u> of the testing done. A score lower than 50 indicates methods and materials which had <u>negative results</u> from testing.

Research-Based Education

I still find it painfully difficult to understand why educated teachers cannot see the obvious failure of these inept methodologies which continue to be implemented year after year! As a curriculum designer and innovator myself - I have conducted, and studied, many implementations of materials that did not work as envisioned. Some succeed later with improvements gained from experimental implementation. Some are shelved. Innovation must be implemented and assessed on a small scale first to see if it works. If successful, then the use of the method or materials can be further improved and polished via on-going trial and assessment with larger groups. The use and improvement of such innovative methods and materials can be gradually increased along with continual assessment until their viability is proven beyond doubt. Only then should they be used on a system-wide scale.

This approach is called research-based education, using materials proven by research to be effective. I am convinced that taxpayers assume this is what is happening in the public schools. It makes sense that they would think this. Surely we have think tanks of experts who compare methods and materials using reliable, standardized testing against control groups to select the most effective tools for our children's education? Whoever believes this must be quite puzzled by the results. In fact, nothing of the sort is taking place! The validation of method seldom plays a part in the selection of materials for millions of students in public schools. Those choices are determined by the progressive education lobby which owns public education through control of teacher colleges, teacher unions, teacher training, and the use of taxpayer provided money to lobby legislators.

Research-Based Education Scale

The Scale on the previous page was designed by the author to assess the efficacy of methods and materials. It should be the standard tool to determine what textbooks and training are used by teachers. **The fact that educators and legislators do not use this, or another such scale, is a total failure of responsibility!** My own materials, proven effective over years of use with thousands of students, would rate but a modest score of 70 on this scale - we have never been able to do larger scale testing on them.

The progressive education methods I discuss in this book score zero on this scale! There is a massive research base *contraindicating* the methods used on millions of our schoolchildren!

Chapter Four
Crisis in the Public Schools

What sorrow for those who say that evil is
good and good is evil, that dark is light
and light is dark, that bitter is sweet
and sweet is bitter.
Isaiah 5:20

Permissiveness was made popular by the child-rearing philosophy of Dr. Spock, among others. It relies on the same philosophical foundations as progressive education. One example of this is the almost complete prohibition of corporal punishment for bad behavior. One hopes this is for the best, but since no comparable consequence for unacceptable conduct has been put in place, problem students have become increasingly numerous, brazen, and disrespectful. Minors go unpunished for serious offenses. Although I do not yearn to return to the days of physical disciple - nowadays even touching a child can sometimes be cause for disciplinary action against a teacher. Teachers sometimes must put up with obscene verbal abuse without recourse. Most will not touch a student even to stop him from beating another student. The adults, having abandoned the field, have put other students in significant danger from increasingly uncontrolled violence. In many schools this danger is already upon us thanks to federal laws pushed by the progressive education lobby.

In 1973, the U.S. Congress passed the Rehabilitation Act followed by the Disabilities Education Act of 1975. Section 504 of the Rehabilitation Act expands the definition of '*disabled*' beyond recognition. Now, students with "*behavioral difficulties*" enjoy civil rights protection and cannot be disciplined for these "*disabilities!*" Section 504 does not set forth a specific definition or set of conditions "*because of the difficulty in ensuring the comprehensiveness of such a list.*" behavioral disability is open-ended.

One guideline as to who might have a "*behavior disability*" includes "*an inability to learn which cannot be explained by intellectual, sensory, or health factors… Inappropriate types of behavior or feeling under normal circumstances.*" It is simple to see how wide open this law is to abuse. **Any student who refuses to learn and behaves badly is, by this guideline, "*behaviorally disabled*' and, once certified as such, legally immune from discipline over his or her behavior no matter how destructive.**

One teacher relates his experience in dealing with students certified as *behaviorally disabled*:

> I'm a teacher - "*Mr. Rossiter*" - at my local junior high, but I don't teach. Instead, I watch helplessly as a small number of students wreak havoc... I've walked miles shadowing my charges while they destroy school property, bang on classroom windows, and scream obscenities to both students and staff... I've seen teenagers who failed all their classes because they refused to open a book. Who smashed a picture frame because they were "*pissed off.*" Who told the school principal to "*go f__k your slutty mother!*" Even with an array of aides it's impossible to prevent this behavior, when "*behaviorally disabled*" students know that no disciplinary measures can be taken. (Rossiter, 2006:p.6)

I am certain there are some readers who imagine this to be a gross exaggeration of some isolated incidents. In actual fact, **students do not have to be *certified*. This hands-off approach has become the norm in many schools!** Here is my story.

Dallas 2004 - The Game

It's 7th period Spanish, The pits! My worst class at Woodrow Wilson High. They are hard to start, as usual. They don't seem to care that their final exam is today. 100 questions, the first 25 are listening comprehension. There is too much noise to even take role. I bang a desk top to get their attention. It takes a while. I launch the test during the lull. I speak out very loud because it's nearly impossible to get everyone quiet at once.

Gradually, they focus on me...and attack! The number of questions on the test provokes a round of vociferous complaints. Too many of these students are talented and seasoned provocateurs. They know that a fairly innocent question posed at just the critical moment when I'm trying to focus attention and begin the test is just as disruptive as a smart aleck question would be at a less opportune moment, and much safer. Of course, the finesse comes in knowing just how much you can get away with. Normally, I will throw them out of my class for gravely disrespectful comments. Today, however, I am under strict orders to contain them in the classroom not only to complete their final but so that they won't disrupt other classes taking finals. It doesn't matter, apparently, that the disruptive presence of certain incorrigibles will destroy the integrity of this classroom, this test, these students...some of whom actually do try. Nope, today they have a blank check on behavior. I cannot throw them out no matter what they do. It is a fact I am very careful to keep hidden from them.

Their criticism expands. "*You need to learn to speak Spanish right. You're saying it wrong!*" I don't respond, with some effort, because my Spanish pronunciation is fine. I sound like a native speaker when I read, not that this student cares. The purpose was to score a point. I announce they will do an evaluation of me and this class afterward. It will not affect their grade, "*Be honest,*" I say and quickly go on. Caught by surprise, comments and complaints are few. Their chance to zing me on this in open repartee is passed. Later they docilely accept the critique sheet as they hand in their test. I have some finesse too. How easily that could have elicited derisive chaos. I asked for criticism, right?

Not that I'm in the clear. They are just warming up. "*How long do we have to listen to you?*" one student asks with a sneer. "*25 questions,*" I reply calmly. At first they call out the answers when they know them. A girl squeals loudly. I call for silence. This has the effect of pouring gasoline on a fire. They smell blood! Several others laugh and take up the high pitched squeal. "*What the hell is that?*" one yells.

Normally all cursing is reprimanded. Forget about sending them to the office, it couldn't hold them all. They are only written up and sent to the office if they curse at me - verbally abusing me with obscenities. This happens almost daily. Of course, it doesn't matter that I send them to the office. They leave my classroom but don't go there. Even when they do they are seldom confronted about the discipline referral that I dutifully fill out with my signature at the bottom and send to the office. The administration may not even read them.

When I check on the disposition of discipline referrals, often their copy of the referral cannot be found. I am amused by the slightly pious way the secretary responds to my query. "*District policy is to give them a 30 minute cooling off period before returning to class.*" This assumes that they have simply lost control in a moment of emotional turmoil. In actual fact, they very coolly and purposefully disrupt in a manner calculated to do the maximum damage to the teacher and the minimum damage to them. For them the 30 minute break is a "*warm-up*" not a "*cooling off*" period. They strut back into the classroom with dramatic disruptive flair. Nothing has been done to them and they are usually emboldened by the experience of being sent to the office for "*discipline!*" Discipline is a joke at this school!

This is the game we play instead of getting an education. It brutalizes the teacher and imparts attitudes that will haunt the students for a lifetime. It's easy to say that you won't treat your boss this way when you get a job but the fact is that they have no idea how to respect others. They only know this game, rooted in their anger at a system that has failed them… and it has! Most have long ago given up on learning anything!

They hate the system - which is society to them. They hate me because I represent that system, that society. I know all this and still I do not hate them, despite the daily humiliation of suffering their abuse without responding in kind. I do it because I am them!

I was worse than most of them, a master of the game. Although I could not get away with nearly so much in my day, still I am them. This experience has made me face something I had seldom given a second thought - all the grief I gave my teachers through my juvenile delinquency. But I was lucky. I changed. Now, the memory leaves me burning with shame at the way I treated my teachers - the meanness, merciless harassment, the application of intelligence to the weak points of the teacher's psyche and procedure. I remember praying to God once as an adolescent, *"Please God, do not make me a teacher!"* He must have heard! I suppose it's my fate although I won't say that I deserve this. My teachers didn't deserve it and neither do I.

For too many of these students, the goal is not to learn but to destroy the process they've come to hate! For the teacher the primary goal is not to educate but simply to survive with some sense of dignity intact. I walk into class playing defense, watching my back. I evade abuse, parry it, let it roll off my back, or...if I have no choice - confront it. Confrontation takes time, energy, and can provoke others. It can backfire! It is to be avoided when possible, not out of cowardice but practicality. A classroom full of constant confrontation is a class where no learning is occurring - just the desperate struggle for control! You lose that struggle, like the last teacher in this class did, and you will dread every minute you must spend in that class. There will be no mercy for you, and on your part only appeasement and surrender, despair and defeat, hate and humiliation, until… sooner or later you walk, just like the last teacher did. You just can't take the abuse any longer. To walk out on a contract means giving up your teaching certificate. You will never teach again - but then again who would want to!

Today I luck out. I find some leverage that works. *"If I declare this test invalid due to widespread cheating and misbehavior you will have to return on Saturday and retake the test!"* "*So will you!*" they say. Not so, I insist. I won't have to supervise their make-up exam. It sounds plausible. Come in on Saturday! The thought percolates. Despite their bravado they really don't want to fail, redo a whole year of Spanish, and suffer the administrative and parental fallout from a major testing meltdown. They size me up with surly sidelong glances. I have been boringly consistent in applying discipline. I see it happen. Without anything being said, all together as if by telepathy, they decide I am for real and settle down. I let my breath out very slowly so they cannot tell that I am bluffing.

They slip into that state that so amazes me, a quiet concentration on the written work. They cannot, will not, listen even to the most useful information. Study is a completely alien concept - but written work they will do. Long years of programming, I assume, dictate that when given a worksheet you must at least put something on it, no matter how pitiful. Yet I have literally given them the answers to quizzes they were taking at the time and they would not listen, would not pay attention, would not stop chatting as if I did not exist.

It is even more profound than that. **I call it the Minimum Effort Theorem.** For example, I prepared a review final exam so that they would be prepared to take this real final exam which is a standardized test. Not only did I prepare this review final but also 5 pages of review notes and grammar, in neat little boxes, just fill in the blanks. I did not give this to them. I display the boxes on the overhead and direct them to make notes from the book where the answers are given, one half of it one day and one half the next. We will quiz on the notes for the review test to make sure they studied them. "*Can't you just give it to us?*" they demand in exasperated tones. I carefully explain that they must write it down so that at least they've looked at it once. "*It's a waste of paper!*" they say, "*Besides, it's already printed in the book.*" I know that if I give them the review handout, few will bother to look at it, much less do the work.

The quiz is when I will give them the neat little boxes with the fill-in-the-blanks. The quizzes are a disaster, of course, nobody studied. Most took shabby notes anyway and wouldn't have taken them at all except they assumed I would grade them on it as was my habit. They have learned that I hold each and every one responsible for each and every assignment, not only doing it but correcting and re-correcting it until it is acceptable or they get a failing grade, no exceptions. Now I return their quizzes and they correct them from the book. For this they receive two quiz grades up to 100 just for correcting their quiz out of the book! Most of them manage to accomplish this although few make 100s because they are determined to dash it off with the least time and attention possible. That is the Minimum Effort Theorem at work. This whole process takes more than a week. Next class period is the test on the review materials.

Every one of the answers to the review test are in the 5 pages of review grammar materials that they have been bludgeoned into writing, quizzing, and correcting. The day arrives and most are not even aware they have a review test despite all the belaboring of the past 10 days. Even the good kids didn't study. Half of them fail the test despite giving them the answers, forcing them to write them down, quizzing them twice and making them correct their quizzes. Minimal Effort!

Now they're taking the final standardized exam, easier than my review test, they say. The class heats up as individuals finish and begin horsing around. Now they know I have no more leverage over them. My options are few. Screaming, demanding, threatening would all be useless and we both know it. Students are moving about the room, lots of loud talk, some playing with cards that I have provided to keep them occupied. I subtly let it be known that any jive excuse will get them a pass out of my room. And if they don't return, I say, just don't get caught while leaving the building. Very few give me an end-of-year goodbye. I am a non-entity to them, a faceless humanoid, a subhuman figure, a scion of the system they hold in contempt.

Maybe I should tell them that I am them! I share their contempt for the needless chaos of the school system that is destroying their future. I know their failure is not their fault but they must take responsibility for repairing their lives now! I don't say this. They would not listen. It would not impact. It would make no difference.

The majority easily pass the oversimplified ACP Spanish test. I'd love to take credit for this as a teaching miracle but half of these kids are Hispanic and some might have passed this simple test the first day of Spanish. They are in my class for an easy grade. I didn't have to bust a gut teaching them, disciplining them, grading tons of papers then regrading them after I make them redo their work. I fought, struggled, worked, cajoled, persuaded them to apply themselves and when the smoke cleared… more than 50% had done all the work I assigned them, another 25% came close. That is a teaching miracle for this class!

I could have coasted, babysat them, given them puffed up grades for doing nothing so they wouldn't complain that I was doing nothing. No one would have objected. No one would even have noticed! That is the norm in so many classrooms - just going through the motions. I was tempted every day as their spiteful sarcasm pushed me into a state of battered despondency. Why didn't I? Without being too noble about it, sitting in the teacher's chair of a class in full-blown uncontrolled riot gives me a headache! But underneath that there is still something else. I quell the riot, establish a semblance of order, struggle to educate even though it seems hopeless, useless and unnoticed because… **I am a teacher!**

This is not an exaggerated perspective. The author has witnessed even worse behavior going undisciplined. **The public school crisis of the coming decades will be students savaging each other without the system having the will to confront them effectively!**

This permissiveness ends at 18 years old when youngsters are put into prison for offenses that previously earned them only a slap on the wrist. **Progressive education has led us to the point where we only discipline our children through the prison system!** There were no *"Columbines"* in previous generations. Now school shootings are horrifyingly commonplace!

The permissiveness of schooling is at odds with the requirements of the job market. In effect, we train children for twelve years in behaviors that are unacceptable in a work environment. In many schools, the child who is habitually late often suffers neither confrontation nor consequence. Standards of dress often conform to the lowest common denominator rather than the highest. Respect for authority is abysmal. The purpose and quality of academic work is lacking. The result is often a *"graduate"* who has few skills and little desire to do a good job, or even show up dressed presentable, and on time. They may come to work with an entitlement attitude, *"Work should be made interesting if you want me to do it!"* There is a tendency to treat the boss with the same lack of respect one previously accorded one's teachers.

Employers' complaints about the quality of the work force coming out of public schools are endless. The vast majority of Americans believe graduates should leave public schools with the skills to work productively. Progressive educators are often more interested in addressing social agendas. A huge amount of emphasis is put upon multi-culturalism even though it is not a significant factor in bettering academic achievement.

Public schools suborn educational achievement to *"natural"* developmentalism which prioritizes the whole child concept - which considers not only the intellectual but also the social, emotional, and cultural aspects of the child's development. Since developmentalists are concerned with the *whole child* and not simply academic achievement, they consider themselves to be on a higher moral level than those who insist on seeing results for the educational dollar. They consider demands for results not only narrow-minded but quite possibly harmful to students' overall well-being. **This presumption of superior morality is often used to justify the atrocious failures resulting from Developmentalism.** Regardless, **depriving a child of the ability to read by using faulty instruction is hardly to be considered morally superior.** The same rhetoric is voiced in rejecting research-based instruction. In short, progressive goals trump educational goals at every stage of the process.

Chapter Five
The 'Progress' of Progressive Reading

*Seeing you have forgotten the law of your God.
I will also forget your children.*
Hosea 4:6

The alphabetic principle has been the foundation of literacy since the Sinai Covenant. That changed within the past century as a result of the progressive education movement. The movement's literacy methods have gone under a variety of names. **Differences in these methods are superficial but their anti-phonics bias is a consistent priority.** They all minimize or reject the use of the alphabetic principle in learning to read. When the public demanded the use of phonics, some were included but half-heartedly, almost never applied corrected and consistently. At times the anti-phonics bias has reached a level of hysteria. **A renowned reading guru once typified the ideal reading teacher by saying "Phonicators need not apply!"** There was, and is, a war against the alphabetic principle in the public schools, teacher colleges, and on-going teacher training.

In 1967, Jeanne Chall, author of *Learning to Read: The Great Debate*, gave a name (*The Great Debate!*) to the ideological struggle of phonics versus wholistic reading that is still raging. Literacy is the crux point in the educational process. Inability to read renders the entire educational process null and void. No science or math program, no matter how well-designed, will succeed well with students who are semi-literate. The drop-out rate in our nation's schools is due to a lack of literacy, but the problem is not limited to drop-outs. **Many graduates of the school system are functionally illiterate as well!** Given twelve years and more than $100,000 each, the system cannot teach many of our students to read well! This is where progressive education policies have taken us. To reclaim our education system we must grasp how it got so degraded in the first place, lest we repeat those mistakes.

In the early 1900s, as John Dewey was churning out progressive educators from the University of Chicago, Edmund Huey published a book entitled *The Psychology and Pedagogy of Reading*. Huey's book supported the Look-Say Method and instantly became the bible of the progressive reading movement. The method involved reading words by sight rather than sounding out the letters. **The premise was that the shape of the word along with context clues were sufficient to guess the meaning.**

The Look-Say Method was often called Wholistic, or Holistic, Reading. **In this new concept of *"Sight Reading,"* sounding out the letters is considered a bad reading habit to be eliminated because it would interfere with the more *'efficient'* process of Holistic Reading.**

Origin of Progressive Reading

After the publication of Huey's book his mentor, Stanley Hall, went so far as to praise the virtues of illiteracy (*"Society needs manual laborers!"*) in order to calm the fears of those teachers who noted that some students simply did not seem to ever find their natural propensity for literacy using Sight Reading. John Dewey, in *School and Society*, inadvertently admits to the superior reading methods of 1915, *"The following states report only 1 child in 1000 between the ages of 10 and 14 as illiterate... It is evident that the public schools will, in a short time, practically eliminate illiteracy."* That prophecy turned out to be false - in its place a nightmare of failure - thanks to John Dewey's role in instituting progressive education over the coming decades.

Iowa was the first state to implement the Look-Say Method on a grand scale. Their schools were soon plagued by reading problems. Dr. Samuel Orton, a neuro-pathologist and professor of psychiatry at Iowa State University, was so disturbed by these problems that he wrote *"The Sight Reading Method of Teaching Reading as a Source of Reading Disability"* for the February 1929 issue of the *Journal of Educational Psychology*. Dr. Orton stated in no uncertain terms that the Sight Method of teaching reading could cause disability and be *"an actual obstacle to reading progress."* He further stated that *"faulty teaching methods may not only prevent acquisition of academic education by children of average capacity but may also give rise to far-reaching damage to their emotional life"* (Orton, 1929).

By 1930, progressive educators were launching a drive to get Look-Say literacy textbooks in every primary classroom in the nation. The NEA Journal published a series of articles on reading instruction by William Scot Gray, *"the most eminent authority in the field of reading."* No other educator had ever been given so much space in the journal. It was, if effect, free advertising for Gray's *Dick and Jane* primers. As a result, within a few short years, the *Dick and Jane* primers had become the dominant reading textbooks in primary schools in America.

Reading Disabilities Arise

Reading problems immediately increased. William Gray wrote another article for the *NEA Journal* as early as June 1931 on how to handle poor readers. Only 10 or 15 years before, illiteracy among school children was practically non-existent.

By April 1935, only five years after the *Dick and Jane* primers became predominant, in an article in the *Elementary English Review*, Gray added a host of new problems causing reading disability. Now there were so many students failing - Gray groups them into categories.

> The types of poor readers may be classified roughly into several groups, namely: non-readers, including those who encounter unusual difficulty in learning to read; those who can read to some extent but who are notably deficient in all phases of reading; those who encounter difficulty primarily in recognition, in comprehension, in rate of reading, or in oral interpretation; and those who are not interested in reading...
> William Gray, 1935, *Elementary English Review*

In October 1936, the *NEA Journal* began a series of articles on reading problems by Arthur Gates and Guy Bond, "*Failure in Reading and Social Adjustment*" (Oct 1936), "*Reading Disabilities*" (Nov 1936), "*Prevention of Disabilities in Reading*" (Dec 1936 & Jan 1937). The articles stated that "*There are probably nearly a half million children in the first four grades of American schools whose educational career is blocked by serious disabilities in reading!*" They acknowledged that inability to read was coupled with "*emotional instability.*"

In only a few short years, Dr. Orton's dire prediction, of pronounced reading disabilities and far-reaching damage to students' emotional life, had happened on a massive scale. Arthur Gates' diagnosis was that primers introduced too many sight words too soon and repeated them too few times. Gates proposed solution to the problem was widely followed. **The never-ending process of watering down the reading curriculum had already begun!**

In the following decades reading books were continually down-graded. Fewer words would be covered each year. Books would be simplified. The number of books for required reading dropped precipitously. For those who remember the *Dick and Jane* primers, it is hard to imagine beginning reading books getting more dumbed down. Yet they did. The *Bill Books* for example.

Why Johnny Can't Read

In World War II, better than 99% of recruits with four years of schooling were able to read at the fourth grade level or more. The 1950 census found 98% of the population over the age of 25 to be literate. Almost all of these adults would have been taught by the Phonics Method predominant when they were school children. **During the Korean War, 17% of recruits failed the fourth grade reading test.** Some of these would have received sight word training which was introduced in the 1930s. By the late 1960s, the Sight Word Method (aka Look-Say) had become common. **During the Vietnam War, more than 40% of military recruits failed the fourth grade reading test!**

Rudolf Flesch's 1955 book, *Why Johnny Can't Read*, briefly sparked a partial return to phonics. Flesch surveyed all the research on phonics versus the Look-Say Method. **Flesch provided evidence of the lack of phonics and the disastrous harm to school children taught by Sight Word reading methods.** Many schools did re-implement phonics during 1950s. The progressive educators waited out the resurgence and within a few years had retaken all of the ground gained by phonics proponents - once public attention was no longer focused on the decline of literacy. By the end of the 1950s, the tide had turned again. In opinion polls, most teachers now professed confidence in Holistic Reading methods. The teacher colleges were increasingly the fiefdom of progressive education, even though research surveys were periodically published demonstrating the failure of Holistic Reading instruction as compared to early, systematic phonics.

Progressive educators never faltered in their continued implementation of Holistic Reading methods even though they had proven to be disastrous! Progressive educators responded with "*new*" methods with new names but no essential differences in the way Holistic Reading was taught. **All the various incarnations of these Holistic Reading methods had progressive education theory as their foundation and a refusal to teach the alphabetic principle as their primary goal!** William Gray passed the torch of the progressive movement to Ken Goodman. Goodman ushered in the latest Holistic Reading method called the Psycholinguistic Method. In the May 1967 *Journal of Reading Specialists*, Goodman called reading nothing more than a '*psycholinguistic guessing game!*" There were few differences between the Psycholinguistic Method and Look-Say. However, changing the name gave Holistic Reading a new lease on life! The Look-Say Method had, by then, been thoroughly discredited by research.

Holistic Reading vs DISTAR Phonics

In 1967, the US Office of Education began the world's largest and longest educational experiment in reading methodology, called *Project Follow Through*. It was a 20-year-long billion-dollar project to determine, once and for all, which reading methods were the most effective. Ken Goodman entered the Psycholinguistic Method under the name of the Tucson Early Education Model. After 20 years and one billion dollars, the winning competitor was an early, systematic phonics program called DISTAR (Direct Instruction Model for Teaching Arithmetic and Reading). The results weren't even close. DISTAR Phonics prevailed in every category by an overwhelming margin! Case closed, right?

The response was an immense flood of progressive education publications condemning the findings of *Project Follow Through* - and criticizing Direct Instruction. Goodman's Psycholinguistic Method (the Tucson Model) - now proven a failure - re-emerged with a new name, the Whole Word Method.

By the 1990s, the Whole Word Method had been supplanted by the Whole Language Method. Whole Language rapidly became universal in the teaching of reading in American schools. In Texas schools it was required that all teachers use Whole Language to teach reading and writing. Whole Language was enshrined in the Texas Essential Elements of Education, which, by law, had to be included in the lesson plans of every teacher in every subject.

Nonetheless, a new US Department of Education report, done by the National Academy of Education (Anderson, 1985), declared that research evidence supported *"explicit phonics."* **"In summary, the purpose of phonics is to teach children the alphabetic principle."** The alphabetic principle was the primary element Holistic Reading refused to teach! The report added that *"If an unfriendly foreign power had attempted to impose on America the mediocre educational performance that exists today, we might well have viewed it as an act of war!"* This echoed sentiments from the National Commission of Excellence in Education in 1983; *A Nation at Risk*, which concluded *"The educational foundations of our society are presently being eroded by a rising tide of mediocrity that threatens our very future as a nation and as a people!"*

In 1988, the state of California mandated the use of Whole Language reading instruction in all California elementary schools. California, at one time, had one of the highest levels of reading achievement in the nation.

After only a few short years of the Whole Language mandate, California literacy rates fell to the lowest of all 50 states. California dropped Whole Language, totally discredited by then. In many schools across the nation, Whole Language was being replaced by the new progressive education reading method, the Balanced Approach of Ray Reutzel and Robert Cooter. It should come as no surprise that the Balanced Approach was not significantly different from its predecessor - Whole Language.

The Balanced Approach to Reading

The Balanced Approach was chosen for the Dallas Reading Plan which was the Dallas ISD's Master Plan for teaching literacy. The Dallas Reading Plan was implemented by Robert Cooter, one of the originators of the Balanced Approach. *"The idea was to train teachers to use a combination of phonics and whole language."* That proved to be a lie, there was no phonics instruction at all. In the first edition of their textbook on the Balanced Approach, called *Teaching Children to Read*, Cooter and Reutzel clearly stated it was based on their *"experience and excitement about Whole Language reading methodology!"* They introduced the term *"phonemic awareness"* as a watered-down substitute but still stubbornly refused to include any early, systematic phonics. Reading methods were now giving lip service to phonics.

Since I was being trained in this methodology by Robert Cooter, I did an in-depth comparison of the Balanced Approach to Whole Language. It showed them to be practically identical with only superficial changes. By the third edition of the book, Whole Language had been disgraced by the free fall of literacy rates in the California implementation. All references to Whole Language were removed from *Teaching Children to Read*. The Balanced Approach itself, however, was not changed in any way. There still was no phonics instruction in the entire textbook. It was, and remains, yet another version of progressive reading methods in a fresh jacket once more. Three years later, literacy rates, already low from the previous Whole language program, dropped a bit further under the Balanced Approach. Of Dallas third graders, 50% could not read a book on a third grade level.

Research shows only 10% of learners who do not become fluent readers in first grade ever attain fluency later! They may learn to read but will often plateau somewhere around 3rd-5th grade level where they encounter longer, more technical words not in their speaking vocabulary. Here their lack of phonics word-attack skills is revealed. These are words they cannot guess.

During the period of the 1990s, in the inner cities of Texas (and most of the nation), only one third of third graders read on grade level. By high school algebra only one third could pass the end-of-year standardized exam, which required significant reading skill. **Only one third of the school population graduated high school!** The truth is that all of this happened in first grade where one third of students did not learn to read well! The public school system succeeded with only one third of the children that came to it, at least in urban areas. In more affluent suburban areas, that statistic was reversed, two thirds of students graduated. However, is 66% passing a statistic for our flagship schools to be proud of?

The Gurus of Progressive Reading

A recent survey of over 800 university professors of education asked them to name the guiding lights of reading theory. They overwhelmingly cited two professors. Frank Smith and Ken Goodman were named as the most influential reading gurus of their lifetime. Both of these men are in the forefront of the progressive education movement. Their positions are the strongest versions of Holistic Reading theory. The editor of Frank Smith's 1978 book, *Reading without Nonsense*, gushed *"The heart of his analysis is the seemingly simple truth that only through reading do children learn to read. Thus the function of a teacher is to act as a guide..."* This is how Frank Smith describes his role as a guide:

> **Decoding to sound just does not work.**
> <u>**You need pay no attention to letters at all...**</u>
> **There are easier ways to identify unfamiliar words.**
>
> (Frank Smith, 1978, pp. 104 & 117)

Ken Goodman, the author of the influential book, *What's Whole in Whole Language?* - came out with a book meant to trump the advocates of phonics, entitled *Phonics Phacts*. This is no time or place to go into a much-needed critique of his book. A simple statement from Goodman should suffice:

> **Not only can we liberate children from letter-by-letter processing of a text, but also we can avoid enslaving them in such a unnatural process in the first place - and <u>that should be our priority as teachers</u>!**
>
> Ken Goodman, 1993, *Phonics Phacts*, p.97)

Goodman's declaration is a perfect reflection of the actual *modus operandi* of the elite of the progressive education movement. While giving lip service to the public demand that they teach phonics, in fact they are attempting to eliminate it from the reading curriculum: *"That should be our priority as teachers... to avoid enslaving... children in letter-by-letter processing of a text!"*

Teachers in the trenches have a pragmatic view and often recognize the importance of the alphabetic principle. Unfortunately, they no longer have much knowledge of phonics. Phonics are seldom taught at teacher colleges, and if so only superficially. Phonics are seldom if ever mentioned in staff development at many, of not most, public schools. Teacher education is conducted by an elite group who select those who join their ranks on the basis of their ideological purity. In their own words, *"Phonicators need not apply!"* **The university tenure system screens out those who do not agree.** Tenure was a system purported to protect freedom of speech but the result has been to create a cabal of like mind.

Indoctrination in Place of Education

For decades, the *"Great Debate"* raged between the supporters of Whole Language and phonics. **Primary research, hard data in controlled studies, always supported phonics without fail!** On the other hand, the number articles, of opinion and criticism, always overwhelmed the controlled studies by a margin of 10 to 1. The secondary opinion pieces always condemned phonics! Tertiary sources, usually curriculum & textbooks, simply presumed that the progressive education methodology was optimal. In short, whenever a tightly controlled experimental study provided hard data that phonics was superior, it was buried by an avalanche of published opinion attacking those results.

Teachers, who do little reading of research literature anyway, usually were exposed only to the publication of opinion promoting Whole Language methodology rather than the hard data contradicting it. Although the advocates of phonics had all the primary research on their side, the Whole Language purists vastly outweighed then in influence and passionate rhetoric. To them, **Whole Language was a revolution to liberate children from the drudgery of the classroom! Research data supporting phonics could be ignored** because the overwhelming majority of education professionals were self-professed progressive educators. That remains true because **teacher colleges have become systems of indoctrination rather than education!**

Most professors have never read the *Humanist Manifesto* and would protest the claim they are implementing its agenda. Their protest is immaterial since the agenda of the left is identical to the secular humanist agenda. The truth is, the far-left agenda has commandeered the secondary education system. In 2002, the Center for the Study of Popular Culture reported that Ivy League professors voted for left-wing candidates over right wing-candidates by more than 8 to 1. Almost twenty years later, the ratio of liberal to conservative professors is now 29 to 1.

Conservative speakers, philosophy, and expression are almost banned from our universities! The extremists among the left routinely trample the free speech of opposing conservative and religious views and have turned much of higher education into a propaganda organ for leftist anti-American rhetoric. The takeover of the education system, by those far left of the mainstream of America values, is a crisis! Now that crisis is inevitably spilling over into the streets in protests and riots.

Thirty Years of Reading Research

In all the decades that Whole Language, and other holistic methods, were the dominant reading approach - **there have been zero controlled studies showing them to be superior!** In 1996 the NICHD (National Institute of Child Health & Development) produced a new, and extensive, survey in which they assessed hard data from 14 research centers, more than one hundred researchers, and thousands of subjects - multiple projects - each project typically of five years duration. The report, published in 1996, was called *Thirty Years of NICHD Research*. It concluded:

> **About 40% of the population have reading problems**
> severe enough to hinder their enjoyment of reading. These problems are generally not developmental and do not diminish over time, but persist into adulthood without appropriate intervention. (NICHD, 1996, Thirty Years of NICHD Research)

The report was the death knell of the Whole Language Method. By way of response, Steve Zemelman, Harvey Daniels, and Marilyn Bizar countered with an article called *Sixty Years of Reading Research - But Who's Listening?* **The article claimed an overwhelming preponderance of hard data research supporting Whole Language.** In the article they relate the story of a phone call from a reporter researching an article on staff development.

When the term *"Whole Language"* comes up - the reporter replies:

"There are no scientific studies that show whole language works!"

There is a brief pause while we silently bid farewell to cordiality. *"Well, actually **there are lots of scientific studies supporting whole language.** As a matter of fact, there are a bunch of them sitting right here on the bookshelf!"*

[the reporter replies] *"But there aren't any studies. It's just opinions. There is no research to back it up."*

Through gritted teeth: *"Are you saying that these shelves are actually empty? That these studies weren't published? We'd be glad to start faxing you some summaries."*

"No, no, no!" Now she is annoyed. *"That can't be real research. People have done scientific research and proved that phonics works, not whole language."*

Within moments our conversation has foundered on the rocks of educational research... in spite of what our reporter friend thinks, **the research overwhelmingly favors holistic, literature-centered approaches to reading. Indeed, the proof is massive and overwhelming!** (Zemelman, et al,, PDK, 1999:p.1)

Zemelman et al, claimed thousands of studies but gave only nine references in the bibliography of the paper. As an Assistant Professor of Education at Texas A & M University, I was engaged in training teachers. Despite the breathtaking arrogance of Zemelman's claim, I was actually delighted to have the references. It is deeply troubling to see ineffective reading methods applied decade after decade to disastrous effect! After all, these are the lives, the future of our children at stake. I had researched the subject thoroughly and was both amazed and disturbed to discover **there was no research base whatsoever for the effectiveness of Holistic Reading**, whether Whole Language or any of its predecessors. It was a relief to find some research supporting it. I proceeded to find all nine of the references cited. One by one they proved to be opinion pieces, lacking in hard data from controlled studies comparing Whole Language with phonics.

I contacted Zemelman and asked him to fax me some summaries of the evidence he had cited, since he had offered to do so for the reporter in the story. Zemelman sent me the same nine references he had given in the article.

I proceeded to research all the references cited in all nine of the articles, several hundred, quite a formidable task. I found only one article worth mentioning. Dr. Ray Reutzel, one of the originators of the Balanced Approach, left his university post for a year to teach first graders using Whole Language! His students scored an average of 93% on the Utah Benchmark Skills Test, 13% above the district norm. This is a good indicator of Reutzel's teaching skills, but nonetheless it also reveals that our reading guru is only a neophyte reading teacher. The lowest score was from *"a boy who knew only a few letters of the alphabet when entering first grade."* **Apparently, this boy, unlike many of the others, did not know the alphabet, or how to read when entering school!**

This study illustrates why Whole Language has managed to survive so long despite its lack of effectiveness. Parents are encouraged to send their children to school *"reading ready."* Educated parents know that is code for sending your child to school **"*reading already!*"**

Practically none of my inner-city first graders came to school reading already. When I question my student teachers or others from affluent neighborhoods - how many of their first graders come to school reading already - the response was generally a surprised, *"They all do!"* Any reading method will work when you have students who read already! They come to school with phonics already taught them by their parents, tutors, or good effective, usually private, pre-school programs.

Early Systematic Phonics

By the 1990s there was a virtual mountain of data early, systematic phonics are the essential key in learning to read well. Less than a decade before there was no consensus of experts. Most educators in the Whole Language movement were still giving lip service to phonics while suppressing its use in the classroom. In 1997, Congress asked the NICHD to work with the Secretary of Education in forming a national panel of reading experts to determine research-based methods of reading instruction. The federally financed survey of literacy studies called the *National Reading Panel* was published in 2000. The survey was a massive undertaking - reviewing thousands of publications and statistical analyses using rigorous research methodology. Its conclusions were the same as those of all previous surveys of reading methodology done in the 20th century - **"*Phonics skills are essential to literacy!*"**

The previous surveys - each comparing dozens up to thousands of experimental studies - are: *30 Years of Reading Research* by the NICHD in 1996; Marilyn Adams - *Beginning to Read* in 1990; Richard Anderson - *Becoming a Nation of Readers* in 1985; The National Commission on Excellence in Education study entitled *A Nation at Risk* in 1983; the massive federal *Project Follow Through* from 1967 until published in 1995; Douglas Carnine - *Survey of Reading* in 1977; Robert Dykstra - *Teaching Reading* in 1973; Jeanne Chall - *Learning to Read: The Great Debate* in 1967; The Louise Gurren and Ann Hughes survey *Intensive Phonics vs Gradual Phonics in Beginning Reading: A Review* in 1965; Rudolf Flesch's surveys in *Why Johnny Can't Read* in 1955; and *Why Johnny Still Can't Read* in 1981.

All these surveys together analyzed thousands of comparative studies of phonics versus the holistic reading methods of progressive education: Sight Word, Look-Say, Psycholinguistic, Whole Word, Whole Language, and Balanced Approach. All of these surveys came to the same conclusion. Phonics are superior! Superior by far, to any other reading method tested. The importance of the National Panel forced politicians to acknowledge that early, systematic phonics are essential to reading success. As a result of the National Panel and its accumulated research, phonics have been re-instated in many school systems and literacy is rising in those places. In many other school districts, Holistic Reading continues to be the norm. Nevertheless, because phonics are used in your district today - it does not mean they will continue to be used tomorrow. The war against the alphabetic principle, and the moral principle of God rages unabated in our nation's classrooms, textbooks, and teacher colleges.

Chapter Six
The Accountability Wars

Do you not know that every word of God will be tested?
Proverbs 30:4-5

One of the classic paradigms in the progressive education agenda is the theory that true learning comes about only through intrinsic motivation, the student's innate interest in the subject. This may be a useful guideline but it is not a truism. The problem is that it is made into a teaching principle - given sufficiently meaningful situations and real-world applications of a subject, student's interest will arise. This vital motive will stimulate them to mastery of the subject. Great when it happens, but one still has to educate students even when many are unmotivated.

Dewey encouraged students to participate in setting the goals of their education. This is still implemented today in certain alternative schools and some *avant-garde* colleges. The student determines what is worthwhile to study - and that becomes their coursework. **This negates a primary value of schooling that it equips students with skills they do not yet recognize are essential to their future!** Students are ill-equipped to dictate what a doctor should know to practice medicine, or even the relevance of algebra or history.

Instead of motivating students, it encourages them to believe their narrow worldview is, or should be, the equal of those who are masters in their fields. It fosters a sense of entitlement, that they need not apply themselves to any study that is dry or difficult. Social promotion is one result of this developmental paradigm. It is assumed that a child who cannot read by the end of first grade has simply not found their intrinsic motivation yet and will later. Holding them back is harmful to their self-esteem and natural development.

Developing self-esteem has become a major thrust of progressive education practices. The giving of medals, ribbons, and certificates - often for negligible accomplishments - is intended to boost students' self-esteem and thereby enhance their performance. Developmentalism encourages teachers to stroke student egos whether or not they accomplish anything worthy of praise. Students are given fancy certificates for being at or above the 50th percentile (the average) on standardized tests. Elementary students cross the stage and receive handfuls of trivial achievement awards and by the end of the ceremony the floor is littered with them.

The attitude of many progressive educators is that if everyone can not get an award then no one should. Many developmentalists oppose grades for elementary school students because it makes the poor students feel inferior. This opposition is extended to honor societies and valedictorian status. Since competition mean many losers, it is better not to compete. Expect little and praise much. **The research on self-esteem is quite the reverse. Students who work hard and achieve well have enhanced self-esteem.** Merely boosting a child's sense of self-satisfaction does not enhance achievement. In international competitions, the U.S. typically comes in very low on academics, yet our students rank number one when measured on their sense of self-satisfaction. **Research shows high performers are seldom entirely satisfied with their efforts, they always seek to do better.**

Grade Inflation & Cheating

Grade inflation is one outcome of the sense of entitlement encouraged by developmentalism. After all, if students are to be praised for anything they are willing to accomplish - giving them easy grades is a part of that. In many schools that I have worked in, teachers can not give grades lower than 50. In one school district I know - no grade is awarded lower than 70. All kinds of accommodations are now being made for students raised in this entitlement atmosphere.

A recent conversation I had with a junior college student illustrated the point. He bragged to me about getting an A in Algebra without even knowing the multiplication tables. I inquired how this could happen. Well, he told me homework in his class was suggested, not required. It was neither collected, checked, or graded. The students were given all the questions for some exams. For other they were allowed a large index card with all the information they could put on it. Some students brought several cheater cards with any problem. The teacher always left the room during the test, thereby allowing the students to cheat, another part of the entitlement mentality. And, of course, they could use calculators.

Survey indicate more than 75% of high school students admit to cheating. In college, the market for internet essays, theses and doctorates on practically any subject is extensive. These excesses have not always been with us. There has always been some cheating but as the exception not the rule. Most teachers and administrators do not encourage cheating but it is to the advantage of schools to turn a blind eye to cheating since it raises test scores.

In the 1990s, Pease Elementary School was the top-rated school in Dallas ISD for five years in a row. Then teachers who inherited their students in later grades began to complain. State monitors were sent in to observe their standardized testing. The school dropped in the ratings from number 1 to number 120 out of 120 schools! A Fort Worth school recently dropped from the number two spot in the district to dead last after monitoring. In the same year, a Houston school dropped from the top 10% of schools in the district to the bottom 10%, their passing rates in reading falling from 96% one year to 37% the next. There is a subtle psychology to cheating. Once the moral boundary has been crossed it gives an easy advantage. That advantage systematically erodes any motivation or willingness to work hard at learning. **That moral boundary can be crossed by a student, a teacher, or sometimes by a school administration!**

It is easy to blame students' lack of character for academic dishonesty, but that is not the author's perspective. We cannot divorce student actions from the poor instruction and moral ambiguity of a progressive education approach that continually touts the importance of learning but avoids the challenge of it. The author has witnessed this moral quandary in many highly motivated, smart, and skilled young people in situations where the instruction is so lacking as to preclude the possibility of success! Students working hard to make good grades and harboring dreams of college and successful careers are suddenly faced with a situation where they cannot win, no matter how hard they try!

Many higher-level classes are taught by teachers who are not qualified in the subject. Unable to effectively teach the subject, the resort to throwing large amounts of homework on the students. These students have only their textbooks and each other to rely on to succeed in the subject. This may work in history but textbooks in more technical subjects like advanced mathematics are very dense - requiring expert instruction to master. **While students must be morally responsible for their actions - we cannot judge them outside of the toxic methodology and humanist philosophy which stranded them in the moral wasteland in the first place!**

Nor can we ignore that there are professionals succumbing to the situational ethics of educational accountability. It is not so much by overt dishonesty. Thankfully, only a small minority of educators participate in cheating. **The system cheats in a different way - through statistical chicanery!**

Standardized Testing

Education reform in the 21st century has seized upon accountability as a magic bullet. Although accountability is essential, the challenge has often been resolved by boosting statistics rather than boosting achievement. As a professional researcher, the author is trained to do analysis of statistical data in numerous ways. Some will put things in a good light - some will not. An investigator needs to see all the data to make an objective assessment, not just the statistics which put a positive spin on test results. For example, in Texas the standardized exam is called the TAKS (Texas Assessment of Knowledge and Skills). The school districts report annually on how many students pass this exam in each grade. The passing rates are impressive, 80% or more. It makes great headlines but few journalists seem to know or care what *passing* means.

When standardized testing was first created for Texas schools, it was called the TAAS test. In order to allow school districts time to gradually improve their performance, the initial passing score was set at 25% the first year with the criterion rising by 5% a year. Note that there are four options on a multiple choice test, so if students had ignored the problems and bubbled in the answers at random most would still pass with 25% or more correct. If a student is guessing, their percentage correct will fall into a range between 10% to 40%. For a testing expert, 40% is the threshold of random chance. Any score below that is meaningless in assessing real knowledge. Six years after the TAAS accountability system was put into effect, the passing score required had inched up to 55%. At this point, a new exam was put into place, the TAKS test, and (you guessed it) the passing criterion was dropped to 25% again, rising by 5% a year. That ploy seems to have been swallowed by everyone concerned. The public was never made aware that the passing percentages were not meaningful. It was simply not reported, thanks to a cooperative press corps, or an astoundingly ignorant one.

One of the most common standardized tests for public schools is the Iowa Test of Basic Skills (ITBS). The Iowa, as it is called, is a norm-referenced test. This means that if 100 students take the test they will be rated on a scale of 1-100th percentile. It is like lining them up with the best scorer first and the worst scorer last. This is a good measure for seeing how well a particular student or group of students, is doing compared to all those in the nation taking the test that year. **The ITBS is useless, however, to show educational progress over time!**

Let us hypothesize the students in next year's test takers literally learned nothing that year. They would still be tested and lined up in percentile rank from 1% to 100%, just like the previous year - despite the fact their achievement was in the gutter! There would be students in the 99th percentile who knew little or nothing compared to the students of the previous year. The test only compares students taking it that year with each other - not relative to previous performances. [**Note: In 2020 this might actually be happening due to the many students missing school for long periods because of the coronavirus Covid 19!**] To get a true perspective, one must have more data, criterion-referenced tests that state specifically what students were taught and how much they mastered. Report cards are supposed to show such mastery but they no longer do because of the tortured nature of grade inflation under progressive education.

School systems typically refuse to release raw data. They only release the spin that makes them look good. For example, given the result that 80% had passed the TAKS test, I would immediately want to look at the average scores. After all, if passing means 40% correct this year - then theoretically all students could have passed without even getting half of the questions right. What has happened to students average scores over the years? Are they going up or down? The most likely answer to that question taken from other indices is that the bottom students are coming up some - and the top students are coming down. In short, we are homogenizing the students at a low level of achievement. It remains a mystery since school districts fight tooth and nail at taxpayer expense, to prevent anyone accessing the raw data that would illustrate the truth of academic achievement. One thing is certain, if those other analyses made the school district look good, they would be released. Since they are not released, one can surmise they are not very favorable. **Percentage passing is a dicey index, especially when the bar for passing is set so low as to be meaningless!**

Such an analysis of test scores does not take into account that questions on the exam and standards that have been steadily degraded over the years. It is sobering to read over exam questions of a century ago and compare then with those of today. The Texas high school senior of today must pass a 10th grade exam to graduate. That exam, however, is at the level of what used to be 8th grade skills only a few decades ago. These standards are intended to be minimum requirements but progressive educators see them as the goal rather than the baseline. This is why the average black high school senior in America reads at an 8th grade level, according to the NAEP. **Many of those students are now teachers.**

Teachers Are Knowledgeable

The author was once part of an elite team of teachers chosen to man the new Learning Centers put in place in Dallas inner-city schools. The Learning Centers were to lack nothing: brand-new buildings, high technology, and the best teachers in the city! These teachers were carefully selected, paid a bonus, and required to take two weeks of additional training. On the first day of that training, the seminar leader asked each table to come up with the qualities of a good teacher. The spokesman for the first group stood up, showed the poster they had made, and announced:

Teachers Are Knowlejable

Not a single teacher in their group caught the spelling error. As you might imagine, the Learning Centers did not cure the low achievement problem. The new holistic reading method, the Balanced Approach was implemented. Since it continued to marginalize phonics, reading scores rapidly dropped even further. The same decline was happening in math education.

Those closest to the problem, teachers, recognize how badly things have gone awry. Teachers are twice as likely as other Americans to put their children in private schools. Surveys show 70% of teachers would do so if they had the means.

The lack of quality in teacher colleges is an open secret among professionals. Education departments are a cash cow for colleges. They are allowed to admit teacher candidates with poor qualifications and little is expected of graduates of those programs. The Education Schools Project recently released a report stating that, of the education applicants to a typical public university, 72% failed the math portion of their entrance exam on the first try.

In many teacher training programs, prospects are allowed to retake the exam until they pass. **Teacher competency exams have been implemented from time to time to ascertain if teachers can pass the same standards they are expected to teach.** The results are usually scandalous with high percentages of teachers failing and having to retake the tests. Teachers unions have been very effective in publicly condemning and shutting down this sort of teacher competency testing.

Statistics of the Educational Testing Service (ETS) back up the contention that teachers typically come from the bottom third of all college applicants. In 1990, ETS compiled the SAT scores of 930,000 teacher hopefuls who had an average score of 864 - at a time when a score of 1,000 was needed to enter most colleges, except for many teacher training programs. ETS ran the same statistical model again in 1997 - there was no improvement in the quality of candidates entering education programs. The same holds true for the Graduate Record Exam (GRE) taken for graduate school entry. Teacher's scores are, on average, the lowest of all graduate students.

In contrast to their poor scores coming into college, grades in education courses are inflated. According to the National Center for Education Statistics, the average grade in education course was an A minus (3.41) while the average grade in science courses was a B minus (2.67). The author, having worked as a Professor of Education, can confirm that many teacher trainees have trouble writing even a single page of effective argumentation based on the criteria of thesis, organization, knowledge, spelling, grammar and logic. Many other critics of education colleges have gone into deep detail documenting this decline.

The critical issue is the lack of effective content in education courses. A "*mathematics*" teacher will get little to no mathematics during a five-year math education program! Mostly they will get methodology courses preaching dubious methods. A new "*reading*" teacher will do little or no required reading of literature, only progressive education training. Teacher candidates that entered college as C students in their high school mathematics do not become better at it. Those who were C students in English literature in high school do not become better at it. **The subject matter which the candidates will soon be teaching are just not a focus of teacher training. What a waste of five extra years of education!** Teachers mainly learn progressive education methods.

The progressive education lobby's answer is to push for advanced degrees and more money for all teachers. This is a long, extremely expensive, and ultimately useless response since teacher training is the problem not the solution. A simple and fairly easy solution would be to require teachers to master the material they are going to teach their students each semester. Jet pilots are required to master the controls and characteristics of any new plane they fly and they do it without complaint. **Teachers' unions howl bloody murder at any attempt to ensure teacher competency!**

There is a reluctance on the part of journalists to dig up the truth of the educational crisis. It is an old story, hardly a scoop. Not only do most readers seem immune to more bad news coming out of the school system, but there is also a collegiality involved. Education writers and editors are often chosen because of their experience in education. In short, most education writers are progressive educators themselves and share belief in the superiority of the methods used in the schools even when the test results do not match their preconceptions. In addition, their access to the school beat is their bread and butter. Writing critical articles instead of glowing puff pieces tends to slam the door on cooperation from the district. Most journalists do little more than publish what is handed to them. The school system has devoted millions of your tax dollars to managing their public image. They spoon feed their spin on test results and accountability issues to journalists, legislators, parents, and taxpayers. When achievement drops they scream for more money!

The Accountability Wars

> With the education mess come the education wars, which also have a life of their own. On one side are the vast majority of educators, administrators, and education specialists. **They all come out of the progressive tradition of John Dewey, and they explain the present system's shortcomings as largely the result of inadequate funding and a reflection of the larger society's inequities!**
>
> (Justin Torres - Fordham Foundation - "*School Wars*")

Accountability is essential for the success of a school system. If you do not know how one school, or group of students, is doing relative to others, then there is no awareness of problems. There is no sense of the severity or possible solutions to problems, which of your efforts are working and which are not working. **Progressive education typically seeks to escape effective assessment for two reasons. One, objective assessments consistently show their methods to be disastrous! Two, standardized testing itself is contrary to their philosophy of education which does not push, challenge, or require much from students.**

On the 2000 National Assessment of Educational Progress (NAEP), only 2% of high school seniors were ranked advanced in science, and 14% ranked proficient. The mathematics scores of seniors were similar with 2% advanced and 16% proficient.

To focus on a specific example, in Washington state an analysis showed that one third of high school graduates were not equipped to enter the workforce. In the Washington study, of those going on to college, 57% had to take remedial courses in reading, writing, or math in community college. A study by the Texas Higher Education Board showed that more than 50% of high school graduates across the state of Texas required remedial courses in college. In Houston, that figure was 62%. The students that go to college are the best educated. What about the others?

In 1993, the U.S. Education Department released the results of a $14,000,000 study entitled *Adult Literacy in America*. They reported that 80 million Americans were functionally illiterate, nearly half the adult population! The report stated that 47% of adult Americans read and write so poorly that it is difficult for them to hold a decent job. A recent United Way survey revealed that 53% of workers in Los Angeles are functionally illiterate. The public schools add more than two million high school graduates who are functionally illiterate every year. Those are the graduates. What about the others?

Hiding the Drop-Out Scandal

During the period of the 1990's, official drop-out statistics recorded a single digit drop-out rate, usually around 5%. A closer look at the figures tell another tale. An average **12,500** students a year entered 9th grade in Dallas ISD, whereas only about **5,500** graduated each year! **This is a 66% drop-out rate, just in high school!** The official statistic given for drop-outs was a per year figure, the current year's drop-out rate not the cumulative figure that would seem most important to know. But even during the four years of high school that would be only a 20% drop-out rate. How does one explain the obvious difference between 12,500 coming in and only 5,500 graduating out? In fact, the drop-out rate included only those students who went into the school office and officially signed the forms that they were dropping out. **Those who simply never went back were never counted.** Of students who did go on to college, one third dropped out in their first year, and another third dropped out before graduating. The bottom line - one third made it through high school, and a third of those made it through college. The NAEP results show only one third of the nation's fourth and eighth graders were proficient in reading and math. This one third success rate shows up repeatedly in the statistics. **The school system hides the fact it succeeds with only about a third of students despite immense time, labor, and expense!**

Since the inception of the Scholastic Achievement Test (SAT) in the 60s, scores have dropped about 20% overall. In the last few decades those declines have leveled off but not risen again. The most significant decline has been among the best of our students. Their competencies have fallen considerably compared to historic levels of achievement. Students at or near the bottom were already hugging zero accomplishment. Students at the top had the most ground to lose. That fact is often overlooked by parents and students who only compare themselves, favorably, to the level of achievement among their peers.

Teachers are contracted to teach what is in their textbooks. As long as the textbooks are watered down or simply filled with incompetent methods and materials nothing can change. I have sat on the textbook committee. The first thing I would do to textbook representatives that appeared before the committee was to ask for their validation statistics. Usually they were surprised. Often they didn't know if there was any testing done of their materials. One rep was prepared with the statistics. They had tested before and after and done an analysis with some pretty impressive statistical methods that said the students had mastered a fair percentage of the skills taught. This is where the non-expert would be awed into silence - but the expert would ask the pertinent question - *"Compared to what?"* There was no control, no comparison to a similar group of students using last year's textbook for example. So these students had learned this percent of skills compared to what? Children who were in a coma all year? Okay they learned something! Good, I hope so. They spent a year with this textbook! Was it any better, or worse, than other choices out there. Validation testing of textbooks without a comparison to a valid control group is almost as bad as no validation testing at all.

What does this mean in practical terms? **We are not producing, nor going to produce in the future, the qualified graduates necessary to maintain the economic strength of our nation!** The cream of professional jobs in this country often go to foreigners, an outcome that has already become the norm. In some critical areas, such as mathematics and computers, more than 50% of professionals are foreigners. We can continue to drain the brainpower of the rest of the world but that does not correct the inherent danger to a nation that cannot prepare its own citizens to handle the critical jobs necessary for the nation's security and economic prosperity. We should all be grateful for these foreigners who have come, and worked, and realized a part of the American dream! **But why can so few of our own children receive an education of sufficient quality to achieve a part the American dream?**

Chapter Seven
The Call from Sinai

*These words, which I command you this day,
shall be in your heart; and you shall
Teach them diligently unto your children!*
Deuteronomy 6:6-7

Success in school generally determines success in life. In my 40 years of experience in the classroom, I have learned a supremely important truth. Success in school occurs within the first day, week, month of a child entering a twelve-year journey. The children who receive good reading instruction succeed. Their success brings enjoyment which stimulates more motivation and dedication to the process of schooling. They tend to like the things they can do well, even when they have to work hard to get there. Most children come to school with an admirable eagerness to learn. The purpose of schooling is to prepare them to be a productive and prosperous member of society. Those traits are engendered right from the start if students have immediate success in learning.

Literacy - the Linchpin of Education

Learning means literacy - the foremost objective of a student's educational odyssey. The sooner students experience success, the sooner they tap into societal goals. **Make no mistake about it - school is society to these children!** They know only their home, their neighborhood, and the school. The school represents the larger world, the greater society. It represents what they are being asked to join and what they are preparing to do with their lives. As they sign onto these societal goals, they begin to think about being firemen, astronauts, or doctors. This starts in the first weeks, or even days, of school! Although their dreams will surely change and evolve, they will be channeled via educational means toward becoming a productive and prosperous member of society. If the process is not interrupted, they will succeed. This can happen in the first weeks of school if they learn to read. **Reading opens doors! It reveals new horizons! No other educational achievement holds a candle to the excitement of literacy!**

There is another scenario! Children enter school and receive poor reading instruction. They do not succeed! As weeks turn into months and they still do not succeed, their frustration grows. They strive to some degree or another, but at some point...

...they stop trying! Frustration turns to desperation then to resignation. They tire of beating their heads against the wall. **This is often the result when reading materials give lip service to phonics, include some but not all of what students need for mastery, and spreading those partial pieces of phonics over three years of schooling!**

In staff development I would always ask the assembled reading teachers one simple question. How many vowel sounds are there in standard American English? There was only one teacher, out of many hundreds, who could ever answer that simple question. There are 15 vowel sounds in English. If you don't know that, and it is not in your textbook - which it isn't - how can you possibly teach students how to read those sounds? There are only five vowel letters. How can you teach 15 sounds? You can't!

Meanwhile our desperate young student is looking all around him at others who have cracked the code all by themselves and are reading but he is not. About 50% can crack the phonics code on their own, all the others need direct instruction. They are not necessarily less intelligent, their brain just needs to understand the steps in the process. The constant messages about the importance of reading (Without the means to get there!) only make the student feel more and more inferior, dysfunctional, broken, a failure! The tenacious ones may continue to strive for years in the face of failure. More likely they give up sooner, having no strategies for attacking words on a page. Without early systematic phonics, they do not know how to begin reading. They stare at the words on the page in despair, eventually in disgust. Sooner or later, without success they will give up.

Once the student gives up, success is still possible, but it becomes more difficult. Children, like all of us really, tend to like doing the things they do well, and dislike doing the things they do not do well. One must interrupt a student's sense of failure and convince them to try again. The method of instruction offered as their new hope must be an effective one! If they do not experience success, more or less immediately, they will turn off immediately. However, in our scenario, **success does not follow subsequent attempts to help them read since the system remediates using the same methods that failed before!** At this point, students turn off and redirect their energies to other purposes. For example, they may act out by talking and goofing around with their classmates rather than attending to any further reading instruction. It is just too painful! Unfortunately, it does not stop there.

Students' sense of failure and inferiority continues to grow while they watch other students advance in their reading, and because of literacy - they shine in their other subjects - all of which require reading. Rather than tapping into the process, our student (tunes out. As his energy is distracted, he receive more negative feedback for not performing or even focusing on the process. Whether the teacher says anything directly or not, the child is now branded a *"bad"* student, at least in his own mind. Over time, usually years, apathy turns to animosity. By middle school, he may become hostile to the entire process of schooling and to his teachers. Remember this is their only concept of the greater society to them. They begin to feel like rejects, outcasts of society.

At this point, a crucial line is crossed. Students who are functionally illiterate may dismiss school and society, and consider themselves apart *and* opposed to it! They have become alienated from the process of preparing for a productive future. Their alienation continues to increase in lockstep with their sense of failure and inferiority. The hostility first rises to the level of *"acting out"* behaviors that display subconscious anger at being cheated of an education. **The honest fact is that they have been cheated!**

The teaching of literacy is a routinely successful process with almost all students when it is done correctly. From that initial success in reading, or the lack of it, flows success or failure in all their other subjects. Students are highly unlikely to be able to perceive this clearly or be capable of expressing it in a more honest and useful way than acting out. Their sense of being cheated is quite well directed even though their anger is not. Our student's bad behavior starts with distraction and, when tolerated, continues with disrespect and escalation. Over time, failing students may continually up the ante of hostile behavior or sink into depression (*"acting in"*) or both. By high school, they may be completely apathetic, head down on the desk sleeping, or actively seek to become expert at provocation and sabotage in the classroom.

A Large Truth - A Simple Formula

Students who do not succeed, first in reading, later in life, often purse destructive options as part of their *acting out* behaviors. In other words, they do it because it is forbidden by society. Their overt acting out is meant to be a slap in the face to the society they have come to dislike, if not detest. They dress, speak, and act to provoke. **The system takes children, bright and eager on their first day, and within a few short years turns them into antisocial miscreants!**

The step-off from that anti-social attitude into criminality is a short one if our student takes it. Students' success, or lack of it, in reading sorts them from the very first weeks of school. The large truth I have discovered is that it is a simple formula. We either channel their energies into productive activities, literacy foremost among them, or they will redirect their energies into other activities which may be destructive to themselves and others.

The channels open for the redirection of students' energies are available on every street corner; alcohol, drugs, gangs, violence, vandalism, crime, promiscuity! They may pull themselves up at any point in the process. Sometimes those who fail in school, get out, get wise, get jobs and enjoy productive lives working in a useful trade. **Seldom do they overcome the sense of inferiority.** With some maturity under their belts they may return to the educational arena and successfully tap back into the process. Many others, however, succumb to the snare of destructive options such as drugs, to medicate their negative feelings about themselves, or criminality because there are few other options available to them. The successful students are typically too busy with productive activities to be overly tempted by these perilous alternatives. Besides, they believe the warnings of society about their dangers.

There is a Solution!

"Hear instruction, and be wise, and refuse it not!"
(Proverbs 8:33)

The continual downgrading of educational standards is exceeded only by the dive in actual achievement! We have all come to accept the current state of affairs as lamentable, but normal. The system accepts, despite their rhetoric, that there will always be a substantial percentage of students who seem incapable of learning. **We cannot end this book on that sad note!** It is fatalistic thinking based upon the progressive education system's unwillingness to implement instruction that produces results. Research-based methods exist and the proof they work has been around for a long time.

The author is a specialist in accelerated learning. I was called from the very pleasant pursuit of teaching English to top executives in Paris, France. I was told to teach students in poor, inner-city public schools. **I was told that the problems were there - and that is where the solutions were to be found!**

I landed in Dallas, Texas, teaching a bilingual second grade class. Half the students would not even focus on the page because they had no idea what to do with the words. These non-readers could not even recite the alphabet, despite the fact many of them started in pre-K and were - therefore - in their fourth year of schooling! I approached the school reading specialist and she informed me that **"They don't need to know the alphabet in order to read!"** Her tone was such that I knew better than to dispute with her. I shut up. That was when I began to suspect that current reading methods were bankrupt.

It did not make any sense, because one thing I knew from the research was that knowledge of the alphabet is the most reliable predictor of success in reading. Further research rapidly revealed to me that phonics was, and still is, the most reliable method of teaching reading to all children. No other method came close to the results obtained by early, systematic phonics. Despite this, there were few good phonics-based materials available, particularly for bilingual classes. The schools were not using phonics so the large textbook publishers were not providing much of it. **I created a curriculum to teach phonics in both Spanish and English. By the end of the year, my second grade students were reading on an average grade level of 3.8, which means the 8th month of third grade.** That was the average, one student read at 8th grade level even in English! Most of them were reading as well in English as in Spanish. The next year I asked for a transfer to teach first grade in order to confront the literacy problem at ground level.

Confronting Literacy at Ground Level

The outcome of the initial first grade class was even more successful. As the result of two particular parents who agitated for a more challenging curriculum for their gifted daughter, **I obtained permission to implement an accelerated learning program for the entire class.** By year's end, 75% of the students ranked above average as measured on the SABE (Spanish Assessment of Basic Education). In both reading and math, 25% were above the 90th percentile of all other students who had taken this test nationwide! Since we had been allowed to use the higher level reading collections, **the majority of my first grade class had completed the first, second, and third grade reading and math materials in both Spanish and English. Thirteen out of twenty students were double-promoted from first grade to third grade!** Results of the first grade bilingual students are on the following chart.

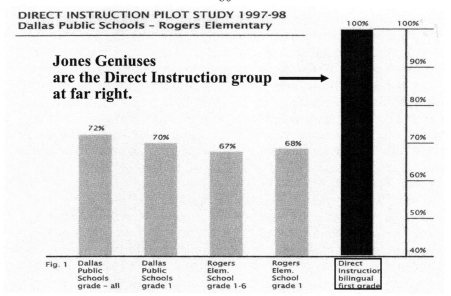

Percent Passing Standardized SABE Reading Test

All students starting the program at the beginning of the year, passed the standardized reading test at year's end. Indeed, 95% of students were above the 50th percentile, and 53% were in the top quarter on the reading exam. On the mathematics test, better than 90% were above the 50th percentile and 56% were in the top quarter in math. The students were also tested in English. The results of the English ITBS Practice Tests, although this was a test which could not be precisely compared to the complete ITBS, it nonetheless indicated **these bilingual students were scoring roughly equivalent to students in English-only classes on measures of reading and mathematics in English.**

The Sad State of Math Education

The Sinai Covenant is a mandate to teach both reading and math. In Hebrew and other languages, the letters were also used as numbers, we still use this idea in Roman numerals - letters used as numbers. The book of Numbers in the Bible is a math primer telling the story of nation building and the mathematics commanded by Yehovah to be mastered by his followers. Progressive education refuses to teach basic skills in math as well as reading. According to the University of Chicago School Mathematics Project published in 2005, **half the states no longer require students to master the multiplication tables!** The National Council of Teachers of Mathematics (NCTM) has been leading this suicidal charge!

In 1983 the NCTM published *Curriculum and Evaluation Standards for School Mathematics*, a document that was to define math standards in the U.S. for a decade. **According to the NCTM, math drills and memorization of math facts were the problem!** Students needed to self-discover math principles and construct their own algorithms for comprehending math. Many math problems should be *"open-ended with not right answer."* For computation skills, a calculator should be used to avoid the unnecessary tedium of learning tables of multiplication, division, etc. According to the NCTM, this would not only improve math performance, but also make mathematics more accessible, *"creating a just society in which women and various ethnic groups enjoy equal opportunities and equitable treatment!"* They called this program Reform Math.

Teachers using Reform Math complained it did not provide enough practice in computation skills and math algorithms. The state of Washington emerged as one of the battle fronts in the *"Math Wars!"* Parent's groups were fighting the state to drop the Reform Math program. By 2002 only 28% of college-bound high school sophomores were proficient at multi-step math solutions, down from 33% in 1990. By the end of the 2004-2005 school year, 52% of seventh graders and 41% of fourth graders failed the statewide math test. Scores nationwide have also been dismal, taking already low achievement down yet another notch! As for the social goals of encouraging women and minorities to study mathematics, there were fewer women taking math majors in college in 2004 than in 1989. There were fewer men as well, of any color.

When attacked, the school system typically circles the wagons. They have the money to lobby and publicize their spin while demonizing parents who want a back-to-basics curriculum! They have lobbyists and experts to speak for their side. Ultimately they hold all the power and control all the money. The school system is a monopoly. Lawmakers are dependent upon teachers' unions for votes and campaign funds. Parents, on the other hand, are hesitant to push too hard while their children are still in the school system under the control of those they are criticizing.

An Experiment in Motivation

An often used rationale for the drop in test scores with progressive education is that we are now including a much broader demographic of students; poor, bilingual, at-risk students. **This *"blame the children"* ploy is only valid if you assume there is something wrong with those children, such that we cannot expect them to achieve at high levels!**

As an experiment, I printed large amounts of practice sheets for addition, subtraction, multiplication, and division. In the accelerated program, we began the teaching of multiplication and division in first grade - not fourth grade as required by state mandates. The majority of first graders mastered all four operations. Mastery meant 100% correct of 100 problems on the math facts test of each skill within five minutes. They had to have two 100s in each skill so that they would not immediately stop practicing those skills.

In order to ascertain whether inner-city at-risk students were willing to work hard they were required to do one sheet a day for homework (front and back, 200 problems in add/sub or mult/div). I announced to my Hispanic first graders that they would be "*allowed*" to do as much homework as they were willing and able to do. They were encouraged to do more than was required but never penalized for not doing so. I have not recorded all of the small successes over the two years, but I hope I have not missed any of the large ones.

Each incident represents one day's voluntary homework:

Recorded Incidences:		Math Problems Completed:
648 times	more than, or equal to	**400** problems handed in
199 times	more than, or equal to	**1000** problems handed in
18 times	more than, or equal to	**2000** problems handed in
1 time	more than, or equal to	**2500** problems handed in

Homework was always taken up daily so it would not be recycled. All papers were spot checked to insure answers were not bogus. In addition, students were tested daily in the classroom and their concentration and motivation were intense! There was no cheating! They were confident, proud and took great pleasure in the competition. **What can you say when shown that inner-city, at-risk first graders are willing to voluntarily do hundreds, or even thousands of problems a day to succeed?**

There is nothing wrong with our children!

The system is at fault!

Did we succeed with all students. One day, toward the end of the second year, while I was calculating these statistics, I noticed that every student in the class of twenty had turned in 1000 math problems at least once during the year, except for three students. I called these three up to my desk and told them that all the other students had done 1000 problems for homework at least once. I gave them the worksheets and asked them if they would be willing to do that as well. I made sure to emphasize they did not have to do it and there would be no punishment, no reprimand whatsoever if they chose not to do it. The next day, two out the three turned in 1000 math problems, one day's voluntary homework. The third student never did. Although he was behind the others he was still competent in all his math operations. Here is a personal story about one such challenging student the first year.

Ivan - A Teacher's Salary

Let's not mince words. Ivan was a woodhead!

Ivan was perhaps the worst student I've ever had in my first grade bilingual classes. Work did not interest him. He had no idea what was going on nor did he care to pay attention and find out. Even when his attention was focused he simply did not understand. Repeated explanations did not change this.

He didn't do his homework. He didn't do his classwork. Even when I put his nose to the grindstone his output was pathetic. His behavior was atrocious! He played, fought, stole and busied himself breaking every rule and enraging me in every way possible. I wanted to break his neck. Inside, I am still just a scrappy little juvenile delinquent on the schoolyard - outraged that Ivan would defy me when I am obviously bigger and stronger than he! As weeks and months passed with no change in Ivan I realized that I would break his neck if I didn't do something about it. So I decided to hug him every time I wanted to wring his neck. It's an unorthodox approach perhaps, especially for me, but I figured at least it would keep me out of jail.

It's not that I don't hug my children. I do, and often despite warnings about the trouble it could bring me, just not when I'm mad. Regularly, I upbraid them for unacceptable work, behavior, or concentration in the strongest language that won't get me fired. Most of these children will face stark choices later.

Their options are not good, menial jobs, hanging on the street corner unable to find work, prison yard, lettuce fields or some other life of equally grinding poverty and misery. I lay it on the line! Spinning sunshine on a stick like cotton candy - won't change these kids' reality. They need an education, it's the only way out! **And I make them work hard for it!** <u>**I am a slavedriver**</u>**!**

For some unfathomable reason these children love me!

Ivan loved me. The hugs did change him although his work didn't improve. God knows what was going on at his house because his smiles were hard to come by. I hugged him a lot since I constantly wanted to strangle him. He still got his reprimands when called for. Slowly but surely he gave up his slow shy smile to me, standing mutely beside me waiting, wanting his portion of affection. He was so small, vulnerable, open like a book, or maybe more like a plant dumbly turning its leaves toward the sun. He became my huggy bear, my "*osito*," regularly melting into my arms. He even began bringing his homework every day and as pitiful as it was he got lots of praise. In January, as the other children raced through their reading and math, Ivan could not put words together and was still counting the dots in his Matrix Math.

Slowly, of course, he did progress. His homework and classwork became acceptable, even if rudimentary. He could actually do some math problems and read some words. **Wow!** Gradually - to my amazement - he continued to progress. Often my jaw dropped when I saw his work. Not only was it acceptable but it was downright good! In a constant state of incredulity I watched his progress; a half page of math, then a full page, performing in his reading group, then performing better than the others in his reading group! He wasn't smart but boy could he concentrate! Just maybe he won't end up in prison!

Some call me cynical, others think me noble for choosing to work in barrio schools when I could command much more money and respect elsewhere. I am not noble. I am what I have always been - a wild child from the wrong side of the tracks. What wisdom I have is wisdom by default. That is to say, having made every mistake in the book and somehow survived I find the choices I have left are usually good and decent ones. **I have become the good soldier** because I can no longer accept sacrificing those I care about for my own selfishness, cowardice, or laziness. I have learned that we humans are one nation greater than its parts or we are nothing more than primitive savages.

Like the good soldier, I instinctively head for the breech in the lines, not because I am a hero but because if I don't we are all lost! I am aware that the breech is the place of sacrifice but, like the millions who sacrificed before me, accolades and a scrap of ribbon or medal are not my motivation. Of course, I am not a soldier. I am a teacher. Teachers do not lose their lives in service, they spend their lives.

The difference is big but not as big as you might think. It is not the ultimate sacrifice but it is a sacrifice nonetheless. I watch as youngsters, with far less education and experience, graduate college and begin jobs starting at double my salary. That hurts! Other professionals frequent stores whose prices make me gasp and live in veritable mansions far from my low-rent barrio apartment. While I have to defer needed dental care because my insurance doesn't cover it - they drive around in shiny new sports cars. My own car, well, we won't talk about that.

Not being able to afford a new car despite being a college-educated professional is minor. Not making enough to pay back the college loans I took to become a teacher is major. The worst is knowing my daughter, a brilliant, hard-working, and highly accomplished senior, cannot go to the top-flight university she slaved for - because I cannot afford it. When my own sacrifice rebounds upon my family - I have the darkest doubts about my path.

Meanwhile, Ivan reads well in Spanish and even better in English! He doesn't have much time left to misbehave because he is too busy concentrating on his work. Today Ivan turned in 2,000 math problems - one day's homework! Ivan now holds the class record in our Homework Hall of Fame for the most voluntary homework in one day.

When all the children were safely off to gym I sat down... and cried! If you don't understand this then you don't understand teachers. Teachers have heart... they are the good soldiers standing in the breech! They know there will be no trumpets to announce their unsung deeds, no medals, no bonuses.

They are our salary - the Ivans of this world!

Results of Basic Skills Practice

In the following year, the author was assigned to teach mathematics to sixth graders. Giving them the same tests in addition, subtraction, multiplication, and division administered to the first graders - the following initial results were obtained from roughly 120 sixth graders in all my classes:

1) Less than half (46%) scored 100% on these basic facts tests

2) 13% failed to achieve a passing score of 70% on one or more

3) Little more than a quarter (26%) could do the tests in 5 minutes

After only **7-10 days of regular practice** in basic skills, two practice sheets a day in class, and two for homework, despite considerable resistance, the following improvements were made:

1) **65% of students were scoring 100s**

2) **Only 5% scored below passing on any test**

3) **58% could now complete the tests in 5 minutes or less**

At this point, the author was transferred to a new assignment. However, in two weeks, even with stiff resistance from students accustomed to doing nothing, much of the skills deficit had been erased by the simple expedient of regular practice.

Meanwhile, the first graders who had been double-promoted ran into problems. One of the third grade teachers did not like the idea of double-promoting these children out of their age level. She did not consider it to be developmentally appropriate. She had five out of the thirteen and **she failed all five at the end of the first six weeks and sent them back to second grade.** This teacher had other students in her third-grade class who could not read at all. In her mind-set, children had no right to rise above their grade level, even if they had already read the third grade books in both Spanish and English. The double-promoted students had already mastered multiplication and division which no other students in her class had begun yet. The parents approached me for help. We eventually filed a federal civil rights complaint against the school, the district, and the state for discrimination against Hispanics in their double promotion policies. Such double promotions were fairly common in the affluent suburbs.

The Godly Yardstick

In the biblical story of Daniel and his companions we are given a Godly yardstick! The blessing of the Sinai Covenant was given in Exodus 35:31 where it promises that those who answer the call will be *"filled with the spirit of God, in wisdom, in understanding, and in knowledge."* That blessing was for men, women, and children as it is repeated almost exactly in Daniel 1:17, *"God gave them knowledge and skill in all learning and wisdom."* When the Chaldean king came to check on their progress, *"In all matters of wisdom and understanding, that the king inquired of them, **he found them ten times better than all the [wise men] that were in his realm!**"* (Daniel 1:20). This Godly yardstick has been ignored because it seems more like a rhetorical flourish rather than anything to be taken seriously. **However, if we are doing education God's way we should not expect an ordinary result - we should expect that the result will be extra-ordinary!**

Negotiation with the school district - over the children double-promoted to third grade and then failed and put back - proved fruitless. The new principal at Rogers Elementary circled the wagons and dug in his heels. I taught the children throughout the summer at my apartment to prepare them for third grade - and continued with them in the Fall - evenings and Saturday mornings.

These children taught me more than I taught them. They exploded every limitation I imagined they might have! Once they had mastered all their operations what does one do with them? Well, as an accelerated learning specialist I knew plenty of ways to enhance their performance - speed reading, memory training, rapid mental calculation. Eventually, I taught them all.

There is a certain point in this kind of training where their abilities suddenly skyrocket through the roof. **At that point the teacher must go with them!** If not then they are a rocket that suddenly runs out of fuel. I remember the first time it happened in the classroom. My first graders were masters of multiplication so I taught them their first advanced calculation method - how to multiply numbers with lots of zeros. It is simple enough. However many zeros there are in both multipliers, add them together and that is how many zeros will be in the answer - 5,000 squared is 25,000,000 and 5,000 cubed is 125,000,000,000. They knew all their squares and cubes already.

We had blackboards that stretched across the wall. I went back to my grading and when I turned around again they had filled the blackboard with calculations of immense size that stretched from wall to wall. They wanted me to check them. I did and they were correct. It was stunning really! How do you go with that? I taught them scientific notation which is really only a method of keeping track of zeros. We moved on to basic algebraic concepts and more advanced mental calculation techniques. Lots of practice.

I was able to do this for the first graders because of my intense study of child prodigies. These young mental calculators fascinated me to no end. I collected their case histories. I was especially interested in the things that triggered their amazing abilities. Sometimes, it was noted how they got started. As I studied these incredible children, their techniques, trials and triumphs - it happened to me! **I was triggered! Suddenly, I found myself doing rapid mental calculation! I don't know any other way to explain it. It just happened all of a sudden!**

It was not a fleeting moment! I was doing it continually in my mind. I carried a calculator in my pocket to check my solutions. I did not sleep much because my mind, my dreams were full of mental activity - **numbers!** When I had to break away to do something else, like work, the numbers were always waiting for me when I was free once more. From the algebra I had in school 15 years before I pieced together equations of how I was doing the calculations mentally. Finally I had to stop doing it because it was obsessive. However, from these notes I put together schemata and penciled worksheets that I simplified and copied for the first graders. They were sort of like magic beans, I think. In any case, they worked. The children thrived on these activities. **Their progress was extra-ordinary!**

The Mensa Contest

During their third month of third grade, the children did a demonstration at a Mensa Conference. Mensa is the high IQ society. There were three PhDs in the Mensa audience and I asked them to form the team for the Mensans. They competed against the elementary school children in a contest of speed and accuracy in calculating powers and roots. **The Mensa PhDs were given electronic calculators. The inner-city barrio children had to do it all in their heads.** Both sides had to write down the question and the answer. Numbers were solicited from the audience so there was no possibility of staging or faking the problems. The winning team had to be first and they had to be correct to gain the point.

The Mensa Contest
Jones Geniuses (Genios) team beat the Mensa PhDs by 14 to 6!

	Problems:	Answers:	Point to:	Time:
1)	35^2	= 1225	Genios	7 seconds
2)	75^2	= 5625	Genios	6 "
3)	125^2	= 15,625	Genios	6 "
4)	$\sqrt[3]{531,441}$	= 81	Genios	13 "
5)	40^3	= 64,000	Mensas	5 "
6)	$\sqrt[3]{658,503}$	= 87	Genios	15 "
7)	855^2	= 731,025	Genios	8 "
8)	$65,500^2$	= 4,290,250,000	Mensas	7 "
9)	109^2	= 10,609	Genios	10 "
10)	107^2	= 11,449	Genios	5 "
11)	1025^2	= 1,050,625	Genios	5 "
12)	$(\sqrt[3]{5832})^2$	= 324	Mensas	13 "
13)	$\sqrt[5]{2,887,174,368}$	= 78	Genios	37 "
14)	$10,035^2$	= 100,701,225	Genios	12 "
15)	$(\sqrt[3]{373,248})^2$	= 5184	Mensas	14 "
16)	$1,000,455^2$	= 1,000,910,206,025	Genios	12 "
17)	$\sqrt[3]{681,472}$	= 88	Mensas	9 "
18)	$75,500^2$	= 5,700,250,000	Genios	7 "
19)	$1,000,955,000^2$	= 1,001,910,912,025,000,000	Genios	18 "
20)	$\sqrt{2704}$	= 52	Mensas	7 "

The penciled worksheets eventually became an accelerated learning program we have used with thousands of children - producing many teams of calculating geniuses. Jones' Geniuses have never lost a competition with parents, teachers, or professors wielding electronic calculators. Would you consider Mensa PhDs as some of the most knowledgeable [wise men] in the kingdom? **Were the barrio children ten times better - as it says in Daniel 1:20 - where it gives the Godly Yardstick?**

You will have to judge that for yourself!

The Call to Homeschool

The well-documented decline in public schools over the past half century has sparked a return to home-schooling. Home-schooling was prevalent throughout this country's history until the imposition of mandatory schooling around the beginning of the 20th century. Even then home-schooling continued, especially in isolated places without schools. An important goal of mandatory schooling has been social - to indoctrinate the values of the nation into immigrants to this country - to Americanize them. Gradually, as we have documented, that indoctrination process has been taken over by the values of secular humanism and progressive education. **They are now indoctrinated to be anti-American!**

The values pushed in the schools today are identical to those of the Humanist Manifesto. They include **the replacement of God's *moral principle* with Humanism** - a rejection of the First Commandment; and **the abandonment of God's *alphabetic principle* - in teaching literacy** - a rejection of the Sinai Covenant. With these two principles gone, the mega-billion dollar public school system has been all but destroyed. Millions of Christians, along with some others, have chosen to pull their children out of government schools and home-school them. I have worked with thousands of home-schoolers. Parents typically refer to home-schooling as a spiritual calling from God. **That is the crux of the call from Sinai. Believers must take personal responsibility for their children's education!**

More than two million students are now home-schooled in the United States, about 2% of the school-age population, increasing by about 5-10% a year. This is about 24% of the size of the **private** school population. Parents home-school for two main reasons; quality of education and religious values. Religious parents no longer believe public schools are willing or able to provide either a quality education or strong moral values.

Parents want their children to have a Christian education or at least an education that is not hostile to their beliefs. At least 70% of parents home-school for these two reasons, usually both. There are other related benefits. They can individualize study for their children to allow them to progress faster or have the freedom to pursue certain subjects in-depth. They have more supervision and guidance of their children's interaction with their peers. They desire a closer family relationship. They fear their children's contact with alcohol, drugs, violence, and promiscuity in the social milieu of public schooling.

Some 5-10% of children in public schools have been home-schooled at one point or another. The reality is not so much two separate systems but a revolving door between home and public schooling. Students often begin schooling and are pulled out, usually because of poor quality instruction. For various reasons these students may return to public schools sometime in the future. Frequently, home-schooled students choose to return during high school because they want the experience of social and extracurricular activities like sports, band, prom, etc. Advanced high school subjects are also the point where parental skills in teaching often fade. If parents cannot afford private schools they may go back to public schools at this point.

Only half of home-school parents have more than a high school education. They tend to make below the median income since only one parent works. They spend about $500 annually per child home-schooled. Although minorities are under-represented in home-schooling - the proportion of blacks, Hispanics, Asians and other minorities is increasing. They are welcome and prevalent in every home-school co-op the author has had contact with.

The term "*home-school*" is somewhat of a misnomer, since they are avid consumers of all types of community classes. They come together in co-ops to share the teaching load or bring in professionals to teach their children. In Texas, home-schoolers are allowed by law to have free copies of the public school textbooks for their child each year. I do not know anyone who has ever actually done so. Why pull your child out of public school only to use a public school curriculum? This has sparked a billion dollar a year market in home-school curriculum. There are home-school book fairs and bookstores throughout the country. These curricula, on-line tutoring services, and co-ops available to home-schoolers are increasingly sophisticated. This support structure enables more and more families to successfully home-school.

About 70% of families consider home-schooling to be a viable option, which is quite a statement of failure of the public schools. The central demographic of home-school families is one that is Caucasian, religious, with the mother at home. This is not to say there are no minorities - there are plenty - but they are the minority. There could be as many as 35 million more potential home-schoolers without exhausting that demographic group.

Since the public schools resist reform, the home-school populace will continue to grow and their network of support continue to improve. Public schools often display hostility or present obstacles to home-schoolers wishing to re-enter the public school system. Universities, however, take note of the higher quality of home-school graduates and are increasingly active in recruiting them. This is especially true of community colleges.

Results of Home-Schooling

There have been numerous studies of home-schooled students. According to data from 2000, home-schoolers scored, on average, in the 87th percentile in reading, 82nd percentile in social studies, and 85th percentile in study skills. Home-school graduates in 2000 scored an average of 1100 on the SAT, 81 points higher than public school graduates.

Home-school students were involved in academic activity 59% of the school day as opposed to 22% for public school students. **Home-schoolers spend more time on task!** As a specialist, this is the most important statistic of all. **It is quite an eye-opener that so little of the public school day is focused on-task, but having been there I know it is so.**

The academic accomplishments of home-schooled children are remarkable:

> **In general, children who are taught by their parents score above national averages on standardized achievement tests...**
>
> Research indicates that the home educated are doing favorably in terms of academic achievement, participation in non-academic activities, measures of social, emotional, and psychological development, and success in college and adulthood.
>
> (Brian Ray, 1997)

Overt hostility toward home-schooling is common in public schools. School districts, teachers' unions, and related special interest groups view them as competition and they continually propagandize, organize, and agitate against home-schooling and voucher programs. They seek to have control over home-schoolers and the curriculum they teach.

Most of all, they want to receive the public monies from school taxes allotted for those students. They advocate a requirement to get permission from the school system, or approval for one's curriculum, before parents can home-school their children. In Arizona, among other places, home-schoolers are required to be registered in an approved on-line tutoring program such as Phoenix Academy. Home-schooling laws vary widely among the states.

Harassment has often been the norm. Truant officers are sent to homes and threats, such as taking children away, or reporting them to state child abuse agencies - are common. At the beginning of the movement, some parents were jailed for home-schooling. Texas has been one of the leaders in fighting for the legal right to home-school. Problems now are more limited to harassment of those who wish to return to public school, putting students back a grade or requiring batteries of testing, etc.

Home-schoolers are torn about demanding their own school tax money for their children's education. Many believe it will come with too many strings attached. Their local school districts want authority over them, their curriculum, and their taxes. **The provision of vouchers could overnight create a market economy for education in place of the monopoly of public schools!** All schools - including public schools - improve with competition!

Voucher programs, where parents have a check for their school tax allotment which they can use for any educational avenue they chose - **will revolutionize education in a major way!** It will undoubtably be chaotic at first. Hopefully, parents will be able to use the voucher for religious schools, private schools, charter schools, or home schooling. **They will have options!** Schools, including public schools, that do not provide quality education will find their classrooms and coffers empty. Competition is already forcing public schools to improve when charter schools open in their district offering a quality alternative education. Local government would still have control to prevent abuses because they provide the school tax monies used to fund the system. **An open market economy for education would work!**

Chapter Eight
Conclusion

The god of this age has blinded the minds
Of unbelievers so they cannot see the light...
2nd Corinthians 4:4

The future of this nation will be determined by the education of our children more than any other factor. We have allowed the public school system to become, almost exclusively, the domain of progressive education. The values of progressive education are, in large part, those of secular humanism. Rather than implementing research-based methods and materials for our children's education - progressive education has foisted upon us an educational agenda disastrous to academic achievement and the social, emotional, and psychological well-being of our children. The documentation of this decline has been extensive and definitive. In certain parts of the school system, particularly at the university level - **education is often secondary to indoctrination!**

In teacher colleges - it is especially acute. Remember that 95% of graduates coming out of teacher colleges identify themselves as progressive educators with values quite contrary to the values of the majority of the population, which are the same general values that they themselves held upon entering university (Stone, 2000). The crisis in education is poorly acknowledged since it is the last thing the establishment wishes to study or call attention to. **Nevertheless, the failure of the public schools must be examined, discussed, debated and confronted!**

The failure to successfully educate students will continue to cost them and us dearly in many ways. Their salaries will be lower - their quality of life impaired. They will be shut out of the best jobs by the better educated, especially foreigners who may work for lower wages. It will cost society as well. Job training costs will skyrocket, as will welfare rolls, homelessness and prisons. This corrupt system is seldom examined by the media. Even worse, **the indoctrination they receive will rip our nation apart!** They have become, in so many cases, anti-American, anti-capitalist, anti-religious, pro-Marxist and/or Socialist. These things have become so ingrained in so many that they will not go away! **They will lead inevitably to civil war, father against son, brother against brother!** I speak of a shooting war not simply of street riots. We will all be caught quite by surprise at how well-armed, organized, trained and prepared the radicals are!

The New Age Zombie Warrior

The school system has created a student ideal for manipulation. They are rebellious to school and society. Even *'successful'* students know there is something disastrously rotten within the education system. They do not know how to think clearly about it. Remember that school represents society to a student. It is all they have known for their entire lives. Critical thinking is no longer part of the system. One would have to weigh different perspectives on the issue, judge the arguments made and the evidence offered to support those arguments. Most especially, one would have to set aside their own bias to see the truth.

This kind of scientific thinking is no longer the norm at university. They now teach what is called *'advocacy research.'* To understand advocacy research, imagine you are a defense attorney defending a client. You will use only the evidence that supports your cause. Any other evidence or point of view will be ignored, denied or even demonized. This is now the kind of thinking that has become ingrained in modern politics. There is no desire to try and understand one's opponent and perhaps compromise on a plan of action. **Not only are your opponents wrong, they are evil! One need not - must not - look at any other point of view nor accept any evidence that does not fit one's own perspective! Truth is no longer a factor in advocacy research!**

So students who are already primed for rebellion against society are spoon fed the utopian ideal of socialism/communism. There will never be an open and honest discussion of capitalism vs communism. Only one viewpoint is predominate in advocacy research. All other ways of looking at the issue are demonized. So today's students are out on the streets of Portland, Seattle, Chicago, or New York fighting the righteous battle to free society from evil capitalism. Anyone who stands against them is evil personified!

They are unwilling to even consider the fact that capitalism has raised billions from poverty - while communism has destroyed every society in which it has been tried. It has proven to be fatally flawed and always entails oppression of the citizenry. **However, to the New Age zombie warrior the end justifies the means!** It is okay, even heroic, to bring down society in order to replace it. It is okay, even commendable, to twist the truth, or just lie, utilize fraudulent ballots, burn, destroy, or even kill - in order to usher in the utopian ideal! **Thanks to their schoolhouse indoctrination, today's students are the perfect zombie stormtroopers!**

It Starts with the Elimination of God

The secularization of the schools is part and parcel of the secularization of the public square in America. Those of religious belief must react to the attempt to eliminate God from the education and public lives of our children. We have become accustomed to sublimating our beliers for the sake of political correctness. There are those who think holding strong religious beliefs should disqualify one from holding high office, such as a Supreme Court justice. There is a movement to erase the strong religious beliefs and symbols of our founding fathers, such as the tablets of the Ten Commandments, that underlie the very basis of our democratic freedoms and institutions. [Of course, now we have mobs of young people in the streets vandalizing and tearing down statues even of Washington, Jefferson, Lincoln and Frederick Douglass!]

In our schools the agenda of the humanist movement has succeeded brilliantly. It has been powerfully re-enforced by the ever more libertine media of television, movies, video games and the internet. **A recent study shows that 70% of children actively engaged in church youth groups abandon church attendance within two years of entering college!**

The Call from Sinai

The Call from Sinai is for believers to take personal responsibility for their children's education. A major social revolution has resulted from those parents who have taken their children out of the public school system to home-school them. They have had to fight the system not only to survive but also to thrive. Home-schooling is still under attach in many quarters, the victim of discriminatory laws and bureaucratic procedures aimed at home-schoolers and intended to preserve the hold of the progressive education monopoly. The home-school movement, however, has the capability to revitalize education in this country for all children. Breaking the monopoly of the public school system is essential. Schools will improve with competition. With educational options - home-schooling, charter schools, and vouchers - competition will rectify much of the entrenched mentality destroying our children.

Answering the spiritual call to take responsibility for our children may mean pulling them out of poor schools to educate them at home. It may mean putting them into a private, on-line, or religious school. It well certainly mean daily help with homework whether they remain in public schools or not. **It definitely means encouraging our children to set far higher standards!**

Answering the Call from Sinai means taking responsibility for educating our children, whatever it takes! Excuses are not acceptable when it comes to the future of our children and our nation. If we do not take back our education system then we will continue to give the best-paying, most challenging and important jobs in our nation to foreigners.

A Godly yardstick demands much more of ourselves and our children. *"Be you therefore perfect, as your Father in heaven is perfect!"* (Matthew 5:48). Striving for excellence is the highest of challenges. Many protest this kind of expectation. Nonetheless, **if we cannot expect excellence then the only thing we can expect is that we will not achieve it! If Hispanic first graders from the barrio can do advanced mental mathematics faster and more accurately than Mensa PhDs armed with calculators - Why should not all our children be equipped with these skills**? A Godly yardstick would demand it. For the sake of our children, and our nation, we need to set our standards higher!

There are schools all over the country that break the mold. One such is Wesley Elementary School in Houston, located in a poor, black, drug-and-crime ridden neighborhood. Under the guidance of **Dr. Thaddeus Lott, Wesley became an exemplary school for more than 20 years with a 100% literacy rate by the end of kindergarten!** Wesley's scores are as high as the best and most affluent schools in Houston. Most important, Wesley tests more of their students than any other school in the district. There are *"exemplary"* schools in Houston ISD who test as few as 60% of their students compared to 90% or better at Wesley.

Dr. Lott had all his children taught early, systematic phonics using SRA Direct Instruction beginning in kindergarten. By the beginning of first grade, all students were reading on entry level second grade, since they had just completed year one of reading. Students advanced more than a grade level in reading every year. By third grade, the typical Wesley student was two years ahead of grade level. **This was despite the fact there had been a 50% turnover of students during those three years.** That means Wesley lost half of their students and admitted an equal number of new students from surrounding low performing schools, many of whom could not read! **No affluent school ever had to deal with such a yearly influx of illiterate students!** Wesley had a great remedial catch-up program of early, systematic phonics. **If it can be done in neighborhoods like the one surrounding Wesley Elementary then it can be done anywhere!**

The author has taught hundreds of children to read using phonics, many of them Hispanics students who, not only learned English but also learned to read perfectly in two languages in first grade! Wesley and schools like it put progressive educators on the defensive. Their success validates the alphabetic principle and reveals holistic methods as bankrupt. Wesley has often been accused of cheating. They have been monitored many times with no substantiation of the charges. Anyone who visits Wesley and witnesses their students' abilities knows this is not the result of cheating. When cheating accusations did not work, funding for Direct Instruction was cut. The Houston Rodeo Association stepped up to cover the costs so the program could continue.

In almost every case where inner-city schools excel, they must fight the system. The Direct Instruction curriculum being used at Wesley was the clear-cut winner of Project Follow Through. Siegfried Englemann, the creator of Direct Instruction, once said he had implemented **more than 100 successful literacy programs in public schools that were eventually cancelled despite superior reading achievement!** Principals rotate, eventually a new one will be appointed who may clear the decks and return to the progressive methods so dear to their hearts. The results of this addiction to mediocrity in our schools are evident everywhere.

The last time I visited Wesley Elementary, Dr. Lott had retired and, the school had a new principal. I knew more about her school and the methods used there than she did. One day, the brilliant light that was Wesley may revert to the dim pale imitation of public education everywhere else. The system will breathe a sign of relief. Wesley will no longer be rocking the boat and making them look bad. I hope not - but I fear it may come to pass!

Parts of the school system continue to successfully turn out well-educated students, but often thoroughly indoctrinated. These students are a relatively small elite mostly composed of those who go to public schools in affluent areas, or magnet schools, those who go to private and religious schools, plus a few outstanding individuals who manage to succeed despite going to mediocre schools.

It is sad to observe high school graduates who cannot do basic reading or the mental math required to make change. We witness with frustration, and perhaps resignation, as even more evidence of low achievement seeps out of the school system despite their efforts to hide, distort, or spin the data.

Yet as I sit writing these words, American young people are excelling at the Olympics! Who can fail to reflect upon the years of dedication, practice, and focused intensity of effort required to compete in the Olympics, much less to win? Which of us is not stirred with pride to see these young people, some only teenagers, strive to be the best in the world? And succeed! Are our children, then, no longer possessed of competitive spirit and a desire to achieve in the intellectual arena? Where are the American winners of the academic Olympics? If we create a system that does not sabotage them, they will succeed! The hard fact is that most Americans no longer expect our schools, and therefore our children, to excel. **By succumbing to this attitude of inaction - we dishonor our children!** We have all the power we need. It is our tax dollars that support the system. **We have only to stand up!**

There is a deep corruption in our public school and university system and it will steal our children from us and indoctrinate them until we will no longer recognize them. **It need not be that way!** We did not start out with radicalized universities, media, institutions, corporation and government bureaucracies of all kinds. **We allowed them to be taken over because we were asleep! Well, we will be awakened soon!** We should not be here in 2020 with our children rioting in the streets - destroying the lives and livelihoods of others! The Call from Sinai, 3500 years ago still echoes in our hearts and minds today, as relevant as it has ever been. We can listen. We can act. **We may not be able to stop the coming civil war but the world is not coming to an end and we must still educate our children of today and tomorrow amid the chaos.** We must reclaim our country - and the education system - and insure this does not happen again.

I remember haunting the hallways of Wesley Elementary to see poor black children from the worst circumstances outperform students from the most affluent schools in America. I saw their proud upturned faces, full of hope, as they relished the challenge. I remember the Hispanic first graders from the barrio going up against Mensa PhDs and beating them. I saw their confidence swell as they mentally computed advanced mathematical problems faster than experts with calculators. In my work with homeschoolers we create an environment where high achievement is the norm. I witness the beaming faces of children of all races as they excel - even though many came into the program far behind. I think of American young people standing on the Olympic podium to receive gold medals for being the best in the world! They tear up, bursting with pride, and I along with them. **This is the real soul of our youth! There is nothing wrong with our children!**

There is nothing wrong with our children! At least until they go through the toxic indoctrination of the public school system and universities. **But if we do not reclaim our country and its education system and other institutions then there is definitely something very wrong with us!**

I will leave you with this final story (and a poem):

The Buck Stops Here!

"*The buck stops here!*" Harry Truman said that. He was a teacher before becoming President of the United States during World War II, the most destructive war in human history - which had already claimed more than 50 million lives! He made a promise to finish the war. In 1945 Truman took responsibility for using the most destructive weapon ever known, the atomic bomb. It took tens of thousands of lives at Hiroshima, and even more at Nagasaki three days later. It is estimated that First Soldier Truman saved the lives and limbs of about a million American soldiers - the casualties we would have suffered in taking Japan. No one doubted the Japanese would fight fanatically to the end. Their survival was at stake. While everyone was busy passing the buck. Truman coined the term, "*The buck stops here!*" He kept his promises. The war was over within days.

Our nation is full of promisers. In every seat of power you will find them in droves - the politicians, spin doctors, and special interest lobbyists whose lucrative professions revolve around promises. Educational bureaucrats make promises as well. They promise that with the taxpayers' money they will give your children an excellent education. I know this because the word "*excellence*" is tossed around so much it seems certain that public school administrators, before being hired, must first pass a test to see how many times they can use the word in a paragraph.

It is a promise unkept. You know this. I could provide data aplenty but I need not quote statistics to convince you that the public school system is failing too many of its students. Despite the millions of dollars of hype put out by the system itself, at your expense, most of you know it is not working. **Why it isn't and what can be done about it - is my theme!**

My school district has a 1 billion dollar annual budget. The entire city's budget is 1.3 billion. This massive dedication of tax dollars is matched in every municipality in the country. The many special interest groups whose lives depend upon the system are engaged in a desperate struggle to maintain the status quo.

These fat cats call it *"reform,"* of course, but it is nothing of the sort, and they will invest millions of your tax dollars in propaganda to convince you they are delivering on their promises. **They will fight fanatically! Their survival is at stake.**

When the promises are not kept then the buck-passing begins. The bureaucrats will scream for more money, find faddish new reforms to try, fudge the statistics, water down the tests some more, find excuses, point the finger of blame at others... It is the fault of the community, the parents, the students themselves, or the teachers. Teachers in the upper grades blame the obviously unprepared students on the lower grade teachers, who blame it on the lowest grade teacher, the first grade teacher... **That would be me. I am their first grade teacher. I accept the responsibility... The buck stops here!**

I make promises too. I promise my children that if they work hard, concentrate, and follow my instruction I will give them the skills to become doctors, lawyers, engineers, and astronauts. I keep my promises. The equation is simple. Either they tap into the educational process and engage themselves in productive activities - or they don't and eventually they occupy themselves with activities that often are negative and destructive of them and others: gangs, drugs, crime, violence, promiscuity - the list goes on.

One must look at all the issues from the inside out, but first let us look at this one issue. **There is nothing wrong with the children!** Granted, I am an accelerated learning specialist but what I do is by the book. Anyone could do it... if they had the right book! I take inner-city children and turn out readers and mathematicians and linguists so reliably that it has become routine to me, nothing of note. All of my children now speak two languages, Spanish and English. They read in both languages above grade level, some far above. All of them know elementary math skills, most have mastered multiplication and division. Not only do the majority know their times tables perfectly but also exponential functions with powers and roots. In fact, they do many advanced mental math calculations faster than someone with a calculator. Today I found myself chiding a young man for taking more than a few seconds to mentally calculate the cube root of a six-digit number. **Then it struck me... I am talking to a first grader!**

There is nothing wrong with the children...
The fault is in the system!

This brings me to the part that is difficult to comprehend, especially for me. **The methods and materials used by the school system have been well proven to be disastrous for a long time now!** There is lots of data and lots of argument but few who think the system is working. The criticism I get on a regular basis is that I am "*out of the curriculum!*" Of course I am out of the curriculum! If I were doing what the other teachers are doing I would be getting the results the other teachers are getting.

What are those results? In university level mathematics in the U.S. now, the majority of graduate students are foreign born and educated. We are not producing American students who can do the heavy academic lifting. I find those students who are proficient enough to take the challenging courses do not want to - because these subjects have been poorly taught and made too difficult to wade through. They opt for an easier path.

The rot in the education system has destroyed the dreams of millions of American children. Many good jobs are now being taken by foreigners. It would be silly to accuse me of being anti-immigrant or racist. My life has been dedicated to teaching immigrants, to opening the door to the American dream - and I do so with pleasure! I am delighted when immigrants come here and find a part of the American dream. I have only one concern. **Is there no part of the American dream left for Americans?**

There is no crisis more important than that being played out today in our nation's schools! The powers-that-be promise the crisis is being confronted and resolved. Yet I feel no sense of crisis coming from the denizens of the school system as I walk the hallways. There is only the mind-numbing destruction of cherished dreams and bright futures - grown so very routine - like the same horror film shown every day until it's grotesque images are mundane, it's ghastly repercussions ignored!

Wars are often not the crises that destroy nations. Most fall from the inside, from a lack of insight or willingness to deal with the problems that confront them. **I have no doubt that the answer to these education questions will determine the fate of our nation!** It is perhaps why I believe that being a first grade teacher is the most important job in the country today.

I will gladly explain why... but for now I must go and prepare for the 22 mostly eager young minds that await me in the morning... for I have promises to keep!

Miles Jones -1997

The Teacher

Take my hand child
I know your daddy's long gone
And your mama's so wild
They put her in jail

I know as you stare
At the seamy sidewalk
Of your tenement there
School doesn't matter

I know, I remember
The red haze of anger
The smell of whiskey
The sight of blood
Broken bottles
Broken promises
Broken hearts

...and the pain
Of those who aren't there
As your daily fare

I know, I remember
Hold my hand tight
That together we might
Go a little closer
Toward that distant light

And maybe one day
You too will say
Take my hand child
I know, I remember
Hold my hand tight
Follow me, follow me
A little closer
Toward that distant light.

Miles Jones - 1998

Appendix A

Book Reviews & Information

Appendix - A

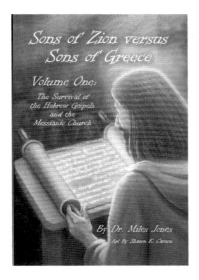

Sons of Zion versus Sons of Greece
Volume One - Survival of The Hebrew Gospels & the Messianic Church

by Dr. Miles R. Jones

Dr. Jones has uncovered the earliest Hebrew manuscript of the Gospels - and authenticated its first century origin! The initial translation of **The Hebrew Gospels** of Matthew, Mark, Luke, and John - reveal a new depth of knowledge of our Hebrew Messiah, Yeshua Ha Mashiach. Heretofore, everything we know about our Hebrew Messiah has come down to us through the Greek filter of a different language, culture, and thought. *Sons of Zion* reveals a secret power given to the Hebrews upon Mt. Sinai, and transferred in some degree to the Greeks. The subsequent history of the transmission of the Word has been the story of the war between the **Sons of Zion vs Sons of Greece**. **The Hebrew Gospels** were carefully preserved, and spread, by the original Messianic Church. Both *The Hebrew Gospels* and the Messianic Church were targeted for extinction by the Greco-Roman Church of Constantine.

This is the untold story of their survival!

Now in publication - go to writingofgod.com
"*Buy the Book*" page to order your copy!

Reader Reviews of *Sons of Zion vs Sons of Greece*:

My mind has been continuously blown/thrilled by what I've read and I have no doubts it will be blown many more times before this final chapter is complete! There is such a beautiful mixture of historical/scientific fact & incredible spiritual revelation in this book! Yehovah bless you for writing this, and sharing this information, and bless the writing of Volume Two! Knowing the history of the early church - the Messianic believers - is something everyone who follows Yeshua needs to know!
Logan

I purchased this book and left a five star review! I'm 2/3s of the way thru it and found it hard to put down. The review was tough to do as there is so much good info, it was hard to describe to the public. A great "Hebrew Roots Primer" or a "Messianic Church Foundational Basics." Your book is truly many things covering cutting edge material for today's Hebraic Messianic Church. I can not imagine the hours of research and effort you put into this book. I can say well done!
Eric

Truth is being made flesh. You are giving me a greater understanding of my roots, a case of lost or mistaken identity. I am excited & can hardly wait for your second volume!
Douglas

Impressive and thought provoking. A confluence of significant biblical issues. Your work and investment to produce this is appreciated. He is Risen!
Ed

I have found your new book extraordinary, amazing & thoroughly scholarly. It has "blown me away"!!!
Paul

The author, by the Grace of God, has produced a valuable work for believers and non believers alike in these end times and has revealed a rare commodity by today's standards, THE TRUTH. Do not think that this book is a boring, dry, "*Religious*" dissertation- it is not. It is a fascinating read!
Arik

You know how a veil can drop, and one can see something in a whole new way, while wondering how it had been there all along and be unseen - like the way you explained the reality and impact of the alphabet being given to humanity at Horeb.
Henry

<u>Raises the standard for research</u>!
Edward

The new updated 2019 edition of
The Writing of God
is also available at: writingofgod.com

When you purchase online via writingofgod.com it does not cost any more than other online outlets but we make three times as much for our ministry, and
we strive to give you faster service
and research updates.

Go to writingofgod.com to order your copy.

If you would like Dr. Jones to come present
to your group now is the time
to schedule an appearance.

email:
milesjns@yahoo.com.

<u>We now have a publishing outlet
in Australia,
so no more exorbitant shipping charges
for our Australian patrons</u>!

First page of ancient text with title overlaid

Sons of Zion vs Sons of Greece

Volume Two:

Messianic Church Reawakening & Recovery of the Received Text

MILES R. JONES
Projected publication date 2021

    The Hebrew Gospels and the Messianic Church had been targeted for extinction - yet they survived and spread! *The Hebrew Gospels* appear again in Medieval Spain along with the resurgence of the Messianic Church among the converted Jews. By the hundreds of thousands Jews converted to Christianity - many were forced - but most converted of their own free will. They shared the same educational traditions as the Jews. They believed the Hebrew story of the Hebrew Messiah should be preserved in the holy tongue - Hebrew. *The Hebrew Gospels* still survived. They were translated into *The Catalan Gospels* and also the Shem Tov *Hebrew Matthew*. The Spanish Inquisition was implemented to crush the resurgent Messianic Church.

    All over Europe and elsewhere the Messianic Church had spread. Pursued by the Inquisition, these Neo-Messianics became the Underground Church and went by many names. There were differences in doctrine but always and everywhere the goal was to restore the original Messianic-Apostolic Church of the first century. They preserved *The Received Text* of the Bible outside of the grasp of the Greco-Roman Church. Many thousands of Messianic believers were tortured and slain. They were never extinguished. Survivors fled to neighboring regions where new churches sprang up. The Neo-Messianic Movement mingled with the blood of the early Jewish Christians - although mostly Gentile now. The Reformation Bibles were recovered from this source. **Within thirty years, two thirds of Europe became Protestant!** The Messianic Movement spread to the New World. The Inquisition followed. They survived and *The Hebrew Gospels* & *The Received Text* of the Bible survived along with them!

Sons of Zion vs Sons of Greece – Volume Two

Chapter Seven
The Golden Age

*The captivity of Jerusalem, which is in Sepharad,
shall possess the cities of the south.*
Obadiah 1:20

Rome fell in 410 AD to Alaric's Visigoths. The Classical Age had come to an end. *"As the Western Empire died, it left behind it empty cities with marble ruins lying like great skeletons at their centres."*[1] The pagan Greeks (and Romans) had many faults but a lack of curiosity of the mind was not one of them. Despite their superstition, the light of reason shone brightly, creating the Western model of science and civilization. The white marble cities were their most visible icon. Now the Dark Ages have begun.

The Roman Church had many good qualities, but freedom of thought was not one of them. The study of Greek and Hebrew were banned. Many priceless classics of the Greeks were lost. For a millennium, the rare scholar who studied Hebrew hastened to declare his intent was solely to expose the lies and perfidy of the Jews. To challenge the dogma of the Church was to court death.

The light came from the East - and it came through Sepharad [Spain]. The term '*Sepharad*' meant '*land of the Book.*' The '*Sephardim*' were, therefore, the '*people of the Book.*' It is true that the diaspora Jews were more Hellenized. Nonetheless, **it was diaspora Jews who would keep both Hebrew language and Greek literature alive for the next thousand years - along with Hebrew Scripture - including** *The Hebrew Gospels*!

In 1971, excavators of the Church of the Holy Sepulcher in Jerusalem broke through a wall, and discovered a room dated to the early second century - when the Messianic Church was still predominate in Israel - but was being forced to emigrate. The excavators discovered a *"red and black drawing of a... sailing vessel with the inscription '*Domine Ivimus - Latin for 'Lord, we went'*.*"[2] Where did they go? **They went across the sea to Sepharad -** '*the New Jerusalem*' **- where the largest community of Jews, and Messianics, was a refuge for emigrants from a century and a half of Roman war against Israel.**

---

[1] John Romer, 1988:p.244, *Testament: The Bible and History.* [2] E. M. Meyers, 1988:p.77, *"Early Judaism and Christianity."* Biblical Archaeology v.51(2).

THE HEBREW GOSPELS PROJECT

The B'nai Emunah Institute has taken on the task of compiling a definitive version of *The Hebrew Gospels* from surviving texts of the Hebrew Manuscript Tradition. *The Hebrew Gospels from Catalonia* [HGC] is the only one surviving text containing all four of the Gospels in Hebrew. There are far too many similarities between the HGC and the *Shem Tov Matthew* [STM] to be a coincidence - and far too few for it to be a copy. It is very clear the HGC & STM both came from a common original Hebrew manuscript. Here are a few, of many, verses which exist in no other version of the Gospel, verses which help lead us to a deeper grasp of the Hebrew Messiah:

In Matthew 1:19 the KJV says Joseph is concerned Mary will be <u>put to shame</u> for becoming pregnant. The HGC & STM say Joseph is worried about Myriam being <u>put to death</u>. In Matthew 13:55 the KJV says "<u>*son of the carpenter*</u>" but both the HGC & STM say Yeshua is the "<u>*son of the smith*</u>" (בן נפח). In Matt 8:5-6 the KJV says a centurion came to Yeshua *"saying my <u>servant</u> lies at home sick."* The HGC & STM say *"my <u>son</u>* (בני) *lies at home sick…"* In Matthew 5:35 the KJV says "*Jerusalem…city of the Great King*" while the HGC and the STM say "<u>*city of God.*</u>" There is a scholia (note) written in the margin of the Codex Sinaiticus of the Greek Septuagint at Matt 5:35 which says *"In the Hebrew Gospel it says <u>city of God</u>."* In Jerome's *Commentary on Matthew,* it says *"the name of <u>Bar Abbas</u> is cited as <u>Bar Raban</u> in the Gospel written according to the Hebrews."* In the HGC he is referred to as <u>Bar Raban</u>. In Matthew 12:42, the KJV says *"The <u>queen of the south</u> shall rise up in judgement."* The HGC & STM say *"The <u>queen of Sheba</u> will rise up in judgement."* In Matthew 28:9 of the KJV *"Jesus met them saying, <u>All Hail</u>."* In the HGC, Yeshua says *"[May] God save you."* - in the STM *"[May] God deliver you."*

SURVIVAL OF A HEBREW MANUSCRIPT TRADITION

The Hebrew Gospels from Catalonia (HGC) and the *Shem Tov Matthew* (STM) were both written in Hebrew in Spain within the span of a century. They are two examples of the Hebrew Manuscript Tradition that survived outside of the hegemony of the Roman Church. Other manuscripts, examplars of a Hebrew Manuscript Tradition have recently been found! The *Cochin Gospels* and New Testament in Hebrew - *The Waldensian Bible - The Catalan Gospels*. The Waldensians were martyred by the Roman Church for millenia for not accepting Rome's authority and interpretation of Scripture. According to their oral tradition, their *Roumant Bible* predated the Latin Vulgate.

I have found markers that designate texts originating from the Hebrew Manuscript Tradition. I am sure that there are more but I only have the Gospel of John in the Roumant Bible to compare at this time. Here are the **three markers:**

1) The name of the Messiah is derived from Hebrew - Yeshuas, Yeshua or Yeshu.

2) Where it says "*son of Man*" in the Vulgate, KJV, etc., it often says "*son of the virgin*" in the HGC and the Roumant Bible (though not in the STM).

3) KJV John 1:1 "*In the beginning was the Word, and the Word was with God, and the Word was God.*"

In the Roumant book of John it says "*In the beginning was the Son, and the Son was with God, and the Son was God.*"

The HGC says "*In the beginning was the Son Eloah, and the Son of El was with El.*"

Appendix B

Benai Emunah Institute Bar Mitzvah Program of Hebrew, Math & Reading

בְּנֵי אֱמוּנָה

B'nai Emunah Institute for Accelerated Learning

The Great Secret

Let us do good to all, but especially to those of the household of faith. Sefer Galatim 6:10

The Great Secret comes from Mount Sinai where believers were admonished to learn the Word and the Writing of God and teach them to their children. Over the centuries, scattered all over the globe, Hebrews rose to positions of prominence, wealth and high achievement in every state, in every profession. In modern times Jews have received 20% of all Nobel Prizes ever granted despite being a fraction of a percent of world population. In the U.S. where Jews are 1.7% of the population, 40% of all Nobel Prizes given to Americans have gone to Jewish-Americans. The good news is that the great secret of their success, the call from Sinai, is for all believers!

B'nai Emunah/Jones Geniuses programs focus on mastering the great secret to help students and parents achieve phenomenal results in mathematics, reading, Hebrew language and history. Our unique accelerated programs and online interactive classes catapult children's learning and take advantage of their marvelous God-given potential. Each program is designed so that you and your children can study at home on your own, or with support online. Our programs are different than traditional learning. We focus on building a strong foundation of basic skills, and then we teach students rapid mental mathematics, speed reading skills and memory techniques. These skills allow our students to progress much, much faster than with a traditional curriculum. By the end of first semester mathematics, most students are able to do math calculations mentally faster than an electronic calculator! No other program teaches children these important mental math, speed reading, and memory skills.

בְּנֵי אֱמוּנָה

Institute for Accelerated Learning

B'nai Emunah - Household of Faith

Let us do good to all, but especially to those of the household of faith. Sefer Galatim 6:10

B'nai Emunah is a non-profit educational & religious institute dedicated to restoring the original Messianic Church of the first century through research and education.

121 Mountain Way Drive, Kerrville, Tx 78028 -
phone 214 546 7893, writingofgod.com

HEBREW INSCRIPTIONS DISCOVERED AT SITE OF MOUNT SINAI IN MIDIAN

The first photographic and video evidence was brought out by Jim & Penny Caldwell in 1992. Since then dozens of books and documentaries have been done on the discovery of the real Mount Sinai in Midian. In 2002, Dr. Miles Jones contacted the Caldwells and they shared with him photographs of ancient inscriptions from the base of Mount Sinai and from Rephidim. The inscriptions from Rephidim were the footprints of the Israelites traced into the stones with an alphabetic caption which said they were the *"soles of their feet,"* written in the oldest alphabet known to linguistic science, the Thamudic alphabet. Four other inscriptions were deciphered by Dr. Jones, all funerary. One said *"Died Amalek"*, another *"Died Hagar"* and another *"Died Amiah daughter of Hagar"* - all written in ancient Hebrew - they tell a story straight from the pages of Exodus! Go to *writingofgod.com* for more information.

Dr. Jones doing field work in Arabia 1990

THE BAR MITZVAH PROGRAM THAT COMES WITH AMAZING RESULTS OF ACCELERATED LEARNING

Believers were admonished from Sinai to master the reading of Hebrew Scripture. That involved numbers and mathematics as well, since the letters were also used as numbers. In truth, Scripture provides us with the keys and the mandate to unlock the entire mechanism of God's universe - math, science, languages & literature. **B'nai Emunah programs** are different than traditional learning programs. **We teach the Word and the Writing of God in Hebrew,** and focus on building a strong foundation of basic skills in math and literacy, then we teach students, of all ages, rapid mental math, speed reading skills and memory techniques. These skills allow our students to progress much faster than with a traditional curriculum. By the end of the first semester of math - students are able to do many advanced math calculations faster than a calculator! No other program teaches students these critical mental math, speed reading, and memory skills.

Do Bar & Bat Mitzvah with B'nai Emunah!

LOST HEBREW GOSPELS DECIPHERED

First page of ancient text with title overlaid

In the turbulent times of Medieval Spain a community of converted Jews dared to restore the Messianic Church of the 1st century - when Yeshua Ha Mashiach and his Apostles still lived. How do we know this? <u>We have their *Hebrew Gospels*</u>! The Spanish Inquisition was begun in 1478 specifically to crush the Messianic Church in Spain. In 1492, King Ferdinand & Queen Isabella completed the Reconquista, removing the last stronghold of Islam at Granada. Immediately they turned to the Jews to expel them from Spain and seize their assets. On the deadline of August 31, 1492 - Columbus' three ships left Spain for the New World filled with Jews fleeing the Edict. Messianics fleeing the Inquisition took *The Hebrew Gospels from Catalonia* with them. They ended up in the Vatican Library bound beneath another Hebrew manuscript, undiscovered for 500 years. Dr. Jones is now translating these lost *Hebrew Gospels*.

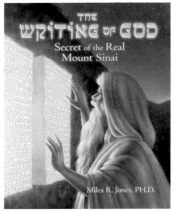

The Writing of God presents proof of the seminal event of the Old Testament, the Sinai Covenant, when God handed down to Moses the Word and the *"writing of God"* (Exodus 32:16). The location of the real Mount Sinai has long been debated. Scripture states it to be in Midian in Arabia where researchers have found stunning archeological evidence of the events of the Exodus, including inscriptions from the base of Mount Sinai.

These inscriptions reveal an incredible secret of the Bible. The *"writing of God"* written by *"the finger of God"* (Ex 31:18) is the first alphabetic writing! The Sinai Covenant was an educational covenant calling the Israelites to read, write, and *"diligently"* educate their children.

The evidence taken from the latest linguistic and archaeological science reveals the origin of the alphabet, the context of writing in the ancient world of 2nd millennium BC, and the importance of the Old Testament as an historically accurate source.

The Writing of God signals the decline of modern education, especially literacy, as a result of abandoning the moral and the alphabetic principle of God in our schools. The call from Sinai is the spiritual clarion call for today's home-schoolers. To order your copy go to *writingofgod.com*.

Jones Geniuses
in the news

For more information
on B'nai Emunah Institute
for Accelerated Learning
go to jonesgeniuses.com
or call 817 718 8822

The Call from Sinai - Ten Keys - Scriptural Basis of Home Schooling

From *The Writing of God* by Dr. Miles Jones

1) The call from Sinai is **a sacred Covenant which God intended to reach the whole world**... *"Now therefore, if you will obey my voice indeed, and keep my covenant then you shall be a peculiar treasure unto me above all people, for all the earth is mine. And you shall be unto me a kingdom of priests..."* (Ex 19:5-6)

2) **It is written by God's own hand**, it could be important... *"And He gave unto Moses, when he had made an end of communing with him upon Mount Sinai, two tablets of testimony, tablets of stone, written with the finger of God."* (Ex 31:18)

3) **The Sinai Covenant is a teaching Covenant**... *"And the LORD said unto Moses, come up to me into the mount, and be there: And I will give you tablets of stone, and a law, and commandments which I have written; that you may teach them."* (Ex 24:12)

4) God stipulates **two purposes of the Covenant, His word and His writing**... *"And the LORD said unto Moses, write these words, for after the purpose and character of these words I have made a covenant with you and with Israel"* (Ex 34:27 Amplified Bible).

5) **God provided the Israelites with a system of writing**... *"And Moses turned, and went down the mount, and the two tablets of the testimony were in his hand: the tablets were written on both their sides; on the one side and on the other were they written. **And the tablets were the work of God, and the writing was the writing of God...**"* (Ex 32:15-16) God specified the writing of God, the alphabet, is of Him. *"I am Alpha and Omega, the beginning and the ending... the first and the last: what you see, write in a book..."* (Rev 1:8-11). The Covenant included numeracy - letters were also used for numbers. *"Take you the sum...and divide..."* and multiply & do fractions & measurement, etc. (Num 1:1).

6) **The Covenant bestows a blessing** on those who answer the call from Sinai... *"And He has filled him with the spirit of God, in wisdom, in understanding, and in knowledge..."* (Ex 35:31) *"And He has put it in his heart that he may teach..."* (Ex 35:34). God specified the power of this Covenant blessing to His believers... *"Behold I make a covenant... I will do marvels, such as have not been done in all the earth... with you"* (Ex 34:10). (continued on next page)

(continued from previous page)

7) **The Covenant is for men... and women**... *"And every able and wise-hearted man in whose mind the Lord had put wisdom and ability, everyone whose heart stirred him up to come to do the work..."* (Ex 36:2) ***"And they came, both men and women, as many as were willing-hearted..."*** (Ex 35:22), **and children**... Daniel and his cohort were learning the word & the writing of God. *"God gave them knowledge and skill in all learning and wisdom..."* (Dan 1:17 also Ex 35:31).

8) **Scripture specifies a Godly Yardstick** - a measure for those receiving the blessing of the Covenant... *"In all matters of wisdom and understanding, that the king inquired of them, he found them **ten times better than all the** [wise men] **that were in his realm**"* (Dan 1:20).

9) **The Covenant commanded believers to teach the word & the writing of God to their children**... *"Said the Lord, I will put my law in their inward parts, and write it in their hearts; and will be their God, and they shall be my people"* (Jer 31:33). *"You shall read this law..."* (Deut 31:11) *"And you shall write them* [words of the law] *upon the posts of your house, and on your gates"* (Deut 6:9). *"And you shalt teach them diligently unto your children, and shall talk of them when you sit in your house, and when you walk by the way, and when you lie down,* and when you rise up" (Deut 6:7).

10) **There is a curse to those who do not obey the Covenant**... *"Behold, I set before you this day a blessing and a curse, a blessing if you obey... and a curse if you will not obey..."* (Deut 11:26-28) *"My people are destroyed for lack of knowledge: because you have rejected knowledge, I will also reject you, that you shalt be no priest to me: seeing you have forgotten the law of your God, I will also forget your children"* (Hos 4:6).

Dr. Miles R. Jones is an internationally renowned expert in accelerated learning of languages, mathematics and memory training - who operates a center for home-schooling. He was called from teaching CEO's and top executives in Europe, the Middle East, the U.S., and Mexico to teach in inner-city schools in Dallas, Tx. He taught in the inner-city for six years before becoming an education professor at Texas A & M.

Previous work as a director of university English programs in the United Arab Emirates and as a specialist with the U.S. government in Yemen training military officers, allowed him to begin his research in the field. As an historical linguist, the origin of the alphabet had always captivated him. There had only been one alphabet in history from which all others are derived. That original alphabet appeared in the path of the Exodus at the time of the Exodus. *The Writing of God* is the culmination of decades of expert research on the origin of the alphabet.

Dr. Jones is now translating the earliest surviving manuscript of *The Hebrew Gospels*. The history of *The Hebrew Gospels* and the Messianic Church throughout history are outlined in his new books:

Sons of Zion vs Sons of Greece - Volume One: (2019)
Survival of the Hebrew Gospels and the Messianic Church

Sons of Zion vs Sons of Greece - Volume Two: (2020)
Messianic Church Reawakening & Recovery of the Received Text

Dr. Jones received his PhD in Foreign Languages & Linguistics at the University of Texas at Austin in 1985. He has taught worldwide and developed accelerated curriculum in various subjects.

THE MENSA CONTEST

In 1995 inner-city Dallas 2nd graders took on MENSA PhDs in a contest of speed and accuracy calculating powers and roots. The 2nd graders did all the math mentally, the PhDs were allowed to use calculators. Teams had to answer first, and correctly to win. We spoke of the Godly Yardstick of Daniel 1:20, where the king stated Daniel and his fellows were *"ten times better than all the wise men in his kingdom."* You be the judge whether Mensa PhDs are some of the most knowledgeable men in the kingdom - and whether these children were *"ten times better!"*

Jones Geniuses Beat Mensa PhDs 14 to 6!

Some of the contest problems!

$107^2 = 11{,}449$

$1025^2 = 1{,}050{,}625$

$(\sqrt[3]{5832})^2 = 324$

$\sqrt[3]{2{,}887{,}174{,}368} = 78$

$10{,}035^2 = 100{,}701{,}225$

$(\sqrt[3]{373{,}248})^2 = 5184$

$1{,}000{,}455^2 = 1{,}000{,}910{,}206{,}025$

$\sqrt[3]{681{,}472} = 88$

$75{,}500^2 = 5{,}700{,}250{,}000$

$1{,}000{,}955{,}000^2 = 1{,}001{,}910{,}912{,}025{,}000{,}000$

Initial Results of Jones Geniuses Accelerated Learning Program

1993-94 L.K. Hall Elementary - Out of 22 second graders, 13 read at or above 3rd grade reading level - 10 read at or above 4th grade, 7 read at or above 5th grade, 5 read at or above 6th grade and 1 read at or above 8th grade. Average - grade 3, 8th month.

1994-95 Sam Houston Elementary - First Grade, 75% were above the 50th percentile on the SABE, 25% above the 90th percentile.

1995-96 John F. Kennedy Learning Center - Sixth Grade, after only 7-10 days of Accelerated Learning, students went from 46% passing on math basic skills tests to 95% passing.

1997-99 Rogers Elementary - First Grade, 95% of students were above the 50th percentile in reading, 53% in the top quartile. In math 90% of students above 50th percentile, 56% in top quartile.

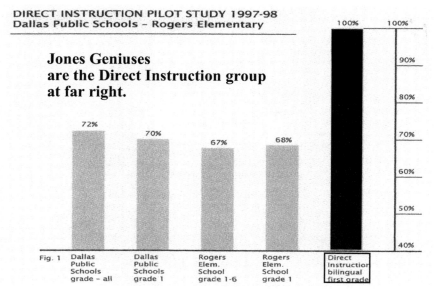

Percent Passing Standardized SABE Reading Test

JONES GENIUSES ACCELERATED EDUCATION

So Many Can't be Wrong!

For more info, go to: jonesgeniuses.com or call 817 718 8822

"Dr. Jones' math curriculum is the most advanced, exciting and easy to implement program I have ever found. The kids excelled quickly and came to enjoy a subject they had only tolerated before. My 3-year-old learned the basic of reading and math. My 17-year-old is doing cube roots in her head. What more can you ask of a course of study?" **Cindy Camp, Garland, Texas**

"The *Genios* regularly stun observers with lightning-fast mathematical calculations. Children are zipping through problems most educated adults would have trouble solving even with a calculator."
Rebecca Rodriguez, Dallas Observer

"I was in my first college math course with students who were several years older than me. On the first day the teacher asked what was the fifth root of 32. Of course, to a Jones Genius that is an easy question, but when I answered it everyone turned to look at me in awe." **Meredith Escobar, Lancaster, Tx**

"Dr. Jones speed reading class definitely helped me obtain a better score on my college entrance exams. Since I have used time-compressed speech for the past three months my reading speed has increased by leaps and bounds. While I was taking the test I was able to skim the reading material quickly and answer the questions correctly. The Speed Reading Lab has definitely helped my reading ability, comprehension and speed." **Cameron Cooper, Austin, Texas**

"Nine months ago none of these children spoke English… Now they are reading Tom Sawyer. First graders now do fourth, fifth, and sixth grade work… A teacher who is making a difference!"
Doug Wilson, Channel Eight News, Dallas

"Kevin is surging into addition and subtraction and phonics. And Maureen 'loves' math. They both love the ribbons. Wow! I'm impressed. Being a math kind of guy myself, I can see the incredible depth of understanding of how the mind learns and the amount of tedious work that has gone into this. I want to encourage you because you are really on to something."
Randle McCaslin, Austin, Texas

"When we first met Dr. Jones, Kristen was in 6th grade and needed a jump-start in math. She was suffering from math phobia and was very behind, barely able to add and subtract, let alone multiply and divide. Within that year she became a Grand Facts Master and her math phobia disappeared. She went on to be on the demonstration team and eventually became captain of the team. I tell people that she went from not being able to multiply to finding the cube root of six-digit numbers. Amazing!" **Tara Rose, DeSoto, Texas**

Dallas Observer
September 4, 1997
article reprinted by the Institute for Accelerated Learning

Are "Jones' Geniuses" too smart for DISD?

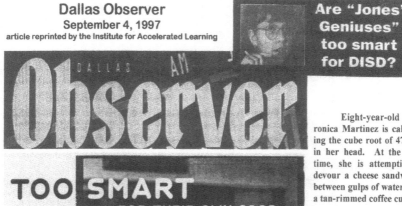

TOO SMART FOR THEIR OWN GOOD

"Jones' Geniuses" can calculate difficult math problems in their heads. But DISD hasn't always liked the answers.

BY REBECA RODRIGUEZ

PHOTOGRAPHS BY MARK GRAHAM

DISD accelerated learning expert Miles Jones teaches his "geniuses" in after-school math sessions, which he sometimes holds in his Oak Lawn apartment. Here he uses handmade flashcards to pose yet another challenge to his elementary-school pupils.

Eight-year-old Veronica Martinez is calculating the cube root of 474,552 in her head. At the same time, she is attempting to devour a cheese sandwich - between gulps of water from a tan-rimmed coffee cup.

It takes less than eight seconds to consume the mathematical problem, slightly longer for the sandwich. She wriggles a hand free and slams it down hard on her bell. "Seventy-eight!" she yells out.

"Seventy-eight what?" asks Miles Jones, her teacher. "Seventy-eight feet," she answers coyly.

Veronica continues to ignore the scratch pad in front of her as she moves on to other problems. Like 75,500 squared. (Answer: 5,700,250,000.) Or the fifth root of 2,887,174,368. (Answer: 78.) Sometimes, as she's working through the numbers in her mind, her eyes glaze over a little through pink plastic glasses. But eventually, the pigtails start swinging, and she smiles again. She's got the answer.

To read the complete article and others, or watch videos of Jones Geniuses go to jonesgeniuses.com.

Revelatory Presentations by Dr. Miles Jones

Speaking engagements are usually a two hour Power Point presentation.
Video portions of many of these presentations **can be seen** by going to
writingofgod.com or on our **YouTube channel**, search for: **Writing of God**.
Contact Dr. Jones at milesjns@yahoo.com to reserve your presentation date.
The suggested topics are arranged by content for Messianic Feast Days:

Purim - first part of the year - a time of celebration of Salvation of the Jews:

Joseph - Proof from the Egyptian Archives of the Amazing Untold Story!
or...
The Great Secret of the Success of the Jews in all Times and Places and How All Believers Can Have this Blessing of Yehovah!

Passover - Spring - The Sacrifice of the Lamb & the Exodus from Egypt:

Inscriptions at Mt. Sinai in Midian tell a Story straight from the Exodus
or...
Where is the Real Mount Sinai & When Did the Exodus Take Place?

Shavout - Spring - giving of the Law at Sinai & the Holy Spirit at Pentecost:

Moses and the Dramatic Secret Revelation from the Real Mount Sinai!
or...
Hebrew - The Earliest Alphabet - The Latest Revelations - Mindblowing!

Rosh Hashanah & Yom Kippur - Fall - New Year & Day of Atonement:

Timeline of the Torah - Scientific Evidence of the Truth of the Bible!
or...
Discovery of Yahweh Stone - Oldest Artifact w' the Name of YHVH!

Sukkot - Feast of Tabernacles - Fall - God descends upon Temple to Dwell:

The Story of the Lost Hebrew Gospels and their Dramatic Revelations!
or...
The Hebrew Gospels - Who Has Been Messing with Scripture?

Hanukkah - Winter - Feast of Rededication of the Temple - Festival of Lights:

The Revelation of Abraham & the Cast of Thousands at Mount Sinai!
or...
Inscriptions from Mount Sinai - Scientific Evidence of the Exodus!